I Can Make You
CONFIDENT

Also by Paul McKenna

I Can Make You Sleep

I Can Make You Thin

I Can Make You Rich

Quit Smoking Today

I Can Make You Thin: 90-Day Success Journal

Change Your Life in Seven Days

I Can Mend Your Broken Heart
(with Hugh Willbourn)

The Hypnotic World of Paul McKenna

I Can Make You
CONFIDENT™

The Power to Go for
Anything You Want!

PAUL McKENNA, PhD

Edited by Michael Neill

STERLING

New York / London
www.sterlingpublishing.com

STERLING and the distinctive Sterling logo are registered trademarks of Sterling Publishing Co., Inc.

Library of Congress Cataloging-in-Publication Data Available

10 9 8 7 6 5 4 3 2 1

Published by Sterling Publishing Co., Inc.
387 Park Avenue South, New York, NY 10016

Distributed in Canada by Sterling Publishing
c/o Canadian Manda Group, 165 Dufferin Street,
Toronto, Ontario, Canada M6K 3H6

Sterling ISBN 978-1-4027-6922-1

For information about custom editions, special sales, premium and corporate purchases, please contact Sterling Special Sales Department at 800-805-5489 or specialsales@sterlingpublishing.com.

For my friend Richard Bandler,

who has made more people

feel good about themselves than

anyone else I know.

Contents

Section Three: Confidence in the Real World

Section Four: The Confidence Clinic

Warning

Do not listen to the CD while driving or operating heavy machinery, or if you suffer from certain neurological disorders including but not limited to epilepsy. If in doubt, consult your doctor.

The information and advice given in this book are designed to help you make informed decisions about your health. It is not intended as a substitute for any treatment that may have been prescribed by your doctor. If you suspect that you have a medical problem, we urge you to consult with your physician.

Important: About the CD

Contained in this book you will find a powerful hypnosis CD that will fill your brain with positive thoughts, confidence, and motivation. Even if you didn't read a single word in this book and only used the CD, you would still notice amazing improvements in your life.

However, I have written this book in a way that plants seeds in your unconscious mind—seeds of confidence, self-belief, and motivation for life. These seeds are then "activated" when you listen to the CD, causing a massive acceleration in your development.

It's best to listen to it when you have about a half hour where you can safely relax completely. As you listen to it regularly, you will reinforce all the changes you are making.

The most important thing to remember is this:

You don't have to believe a single word I say.

Just read the book, follow my instructions, and use the CD every day for at least a week and your life will dramatically improve!

1

Prepare for Success!

Are you living up to your full potential?

Not one of the hundreds of thousands of people I've worked with over the years believes that they are—and they're right. Even the business leaders, Hollywood stars, and Olympic champions I've worked with who were at the top of their game knew that they were only tapping into a part of what we are all truly capable of being, doing, and having.

Study after study has revealed that there is as little as a 1 percent difference between being a champion and an also-ran in athletic performance—and I believe the difference that makes that difference is confidence.

I Can Make You Confident is not just a book—it's a system designed to give you the edge in every area of your life. As you do the exercises and follow my instructions throughout this book and on the accompanying CD, you will become significantly better at whatever it is that you do. You will begin to notice yourself enjoying your life more, and you will find challenges that once seemed insurmountable become insignificant in the face of your new levels of confidence. Together, we are going to program your mind for success and condition you to become everything you have ever wanted to be.

What I can tell you for certain is this—it doesn't matter how things are in your life right now, how long you have been the way you are, or even if you're skeptical about how well this will work for you. It can all change in a day. And that day is today!

How This Book Works

Using this system is like doing a series of personal sessions with me. Everything you need to succeed is inside this book, including a CD that will help you reprogram your mind for greater confidence and motivation every single day of your life. Soon, you will be tapping into your full potential and using your natural confidence to create the life you really want to live.

Each of the four main sections in this book will take you step by step from wherever you are to wherever you want to be. Section One, "Developing the Confidence Habit," is like sitting down with me in my office. Together, we will go through a series of sessions designed to systematically boost your confidence until feelings of ease and well-being are your natural response to the things that used to bother you.

By the time you've finished with Section One, your life will already feel different. You will see new possibilities where before there were only obstacles. You will have learned how to use your amazing mind to create states of powerful self-confidence and intense motivation at the push of a psychological switch. You will be more comfortable in your own skin than ever before.

In Section Two, "Motivate Yourself for Success," I will share the secrets of highly motivated people. Before we finish our time together in this section, you will be filled with the desire to go out into the world and take massive action to make your dreams come true. More than that, you will feel relaxed and energized as you do so, knowing that you have prepared as best you can and are ready to test yourself in the only arena that counts—your one and only life.

Section Three, "Confidence in the Real World," is like sitting in on one of my success seminars. While you're welcome to read Section Three straight through to the end, I've designed it as a reference manual for real-world success. You can dip in and begin with just the sections you most want to master, whether the changes you really want to make are in your business, social situations, public speaking, or even intimate relationships.

Finally, in Section Four, "The Confidence Clinic," I will deal with some of the most frequently asked questions which come up when people are first learning to master their internal world, unleash their natural confidence, and get into action.

What You Need to Know Before We Begin

Imagine that you've just hired me to help you to become more confident and motivated to go for anything you want in life. What would you most want to change? What would you want to use me to do?

Since by buying this book you have effectively hired me as your success coach, there are a few things you need to know before we get started:

1. I am an extremely diligent employee

When I work with my clients, I am relentless in ensuring that they get everything they need and more from our time together. In order to assist you in fulfilling your potential, I will not just be working with you—I will be speaking directly with your unconscious mind, the part of you that ultimately controls every aspect of your behavior. It keeps your heart beating, your brain thinking, and your body regenerating.

Throughout this book, I will be instructing your unconscious mind to get you to go out and do new things. If that sounds a bit frightening at first, it's because you know that now is the time to do something different for a change. As Einstein said, the definition of insanity is to keep doing the same things over and over again and expecting a different result.

There may even be times when things I suggest bring up uncomfortable feelings or challenge your old ways of thinking. If that happens for you, it is a very good sign. After all, it was your old ways of thinking that kept you stuck in many areas of your life. And if your worldview feels threatened by something I've said, that just means the process of unconscious change has already begun.

2. This book is different

Each chapter in this book is a distillation of what I've learned and practiced over thousands of hours of working with people just like you. This information took me years to assemble, and even longer to put into the most concise form possible. Each chapter is deliberately short, sharp, and to the point.

Because of this, it will take you just a few minutes to benefit from each chapter and, if you choose, you can go through the entire book in just a few hours.

But even though you may surprise yourself by how quickly things change for the better as you read, keep using the CD for several weeks afterwards to reinforce your newly emerging levels of confidence and motivation. Each of the suggestions that fill these pages and the exercises you will be doing are designed to be activated by the CD. Together, the book, exercises, and CD make up a complete system for unleashing your natural confidence and getting you into action.

3. I will be with you every step of the way

As your attitudes about yourself and your life become more self-assured, the people around you will begin perceiving and treating you in new ways. Sometimes you will be aware of the increased positive energy you are exuding while at other times you will simply notice people commenting on how you seem more relaxed, happier, more confident, or that there's something "different" about you.

But our journey together doesn't end when you finish reading this book. By listening to the CD each day and referring back to sections of the book, you will be able to give yourself an instant boost of confidence and well-being every single day of your life.

Who Are You Becoming?

Perhaps the most important principle you will learn throughout this book is this:

What you practice, you become.

Most people have spent their lives practicing stopping themselves from going for what they want and then beating themselves up about doing such a good job of it. They have become experts at not taking action and then justifying their apparent failure by convincing themselves that there must be something wrong with them. Yet nothing could be further from the truth.

The reason people fail is not because there's something wrong with them—it's because failure is part of the process of success.

To high achievers, failure doesn't mean "it's time to give up"—it means it's time to step back, learn from what happened, and recognize that you're now more prepared to succeed than ever before. Actor Mel Gibson calls failure "school fees"—the price you pay for the life you want to live.

But even though mistakes and failures are ever-present steppingstones on your journey to success, they needn't prevent you from getting started. As the Chinese say, "The journey of a thousand miles begins with a single step." And your first step begins the moment you turn the page . . .

Developing the Confidence Habit

Prepare Yourself for Success

Natural Confidence

Have you ever heard someone say about a person "they seem comfortable in their own skin"?

> *"Don't compromise yourself—you are all you've got."*
>
> JANIS JOPLIN

This is the essence of natural confidence—feeling a level of comfort with yourself that can withstand the slings and arrows of outrageous fortune and carry you forward to the life of your dreams.

This type of confidence is not something that some people are born with and others will never attain—it is the inevitable result of taking a few daily actions on a consistent basis. It is a process that you have already begun simply by picking up this book.

Stop for a moment and vividly imagine how your life would be if you were already naturally confident right now—at ease with yourself and whatever is going on around you:

- *How would your posture be?*

- *How would your voice sound?*

- *What kinds of things would you be saying to yourself?*

- *What would you picture in your mind?*

If you actually took the time to imagine any of these things, chances are you are already feeling more confident than you were just a few short moments ago.

But as you will soon be learning, confidence is much more than just a positive feeling in your body—it's an attitude and approach to life that leads to success, motivation, and new possibilities!

You Already Know What to Do

I never cease to be amazed at the number of people who come up to me and say, "I'm just not a confident person." When I ask them if they're sure about that, they boldly declare, "Of course I am!"

The problem isn't that they lack confidence—it's that they're confident about the wrong things. In fact, they're supremely confident about the idea that they have no confidence.

> "We are what we repeatedly do. Excellence then is not an act, but a habit."
> ARISTOTLE

Wouldn't it be great instead to automatically go into your most confident and resourceful emotional states whenever you needed them most?

Imagine being able to step in front of a group or up onto a stage and feel even more confident than you did when you were sitting on the sidelines. Or finding yourself becoming noticeably more confident with each step as you approach an attractive person to ask them out on a date.

If this sounds impossible to you or even too good to be true, you're in for a pleasant surprise. You are already an expert at the skills you will be using to develop the confidence habit.

Think about it—do you ever forget to become nervous before approaching someone you're attracted to? Ever slip up and not feel uncomfortable before making a presentation or an important phone call for work?

Remember, our core principle is this:

What you practice, you become.

Some people have practiced going into an unre-sourceful state before giving a presentation or asking someone out on a date so many times that they now automatically feel scared when they come to do it. They may even have begun to think of themselves as extremely un-confident people.

In contrast, high achievers have often been faced with situations that involve risk and uncertainty.

Because they have practiced putting themselves into resourceful states and taking action, embracing risk and uncertainty in difficult situations has become their habit. They have become completely comfortable in their own skins—and you can too!

The Vibration of Success

Imagine I have two violins. When I play a note on one of them, the corresponding string on the other violin will vibrate as well. Scientists call this "the law of sympathetic resonance"—the phenomenon whereby whenever two objects are tuned to the same frequency, the energy from one is automatically transferred to the other.

> "On an energy level there is no giving or receiving—just energy moving around within itself."
> STUART WILDE

Because the human body is composed of a complex system of high-tech electric currents and electromagnetic fields, the same thing happens with people. In fact, phrases such as "being in tune," "feeling connected," and "being on the same wavelength" are attempts at describing the way energy naturally moves back and forth between two or more bodies.

As you practice these techniques, you are changing your resonance and vibrating at a different frequency. You will become more attractive to the people and things you really want in your life. And as you attract more happiness and success into your life, your energy will continue to change for the better.

The Gradual Confidence Booster

Would you like to feel noticeably more confident in the next few minutes?

Every year, thousands of people run in a marathon somewhere in the world for the first time. But

> "A jug fills drop by drop."
> THE BUDDHA

unless you are in amazing physical shape to begin with, you wouldn't expect to be able to go out and run twenty-six-plus miles on your first try. If you haven't been exercising regularly, you may find it difficult at first to go out and run even one mile.

So you would have to approach your target gradually, step by step. For the first week you might aim to run one mile a day. The next week, you'd do a few miles. Eventually, you'd be able to run ten. Your next milestone would be a half-marathon—approximately thirteen miles.

Then one day, all of a sudden, you would find yourself able to run a full twenty-six-mile marathon the same way the greatest runners in the world do it—one mile at a time.

This is how you will develop the confidence habit. If I asked you to imagine yourself as being more confident right now, you would only be able to do this from within the limits of what you have done up until now—your habitual confidence preset. But by doing it in stages, step by step, you will be amazed at your ability to go beyond your previous limitations and feel absolutely fantastic . . .

The Gradual Confidence Booster

Read through the exercise before you do it for the first time . . .

1. Imagine a slightly more confident you sitting or standing in front of you.

2. Now, I'd like you to imagine stepping in to that more confident you. See through their eyes, hear through their ears and feel the feelings of your more confident self. And notice that right in front of you is an even more confident you—sitting or standing a little bit taller, a look of slightly more self-belief behind their eyes, emanating a little bit of extra charisma.

3. Step into this more confident self, and notice that in front of you is an even more confident self—more passion, more power, more ease, more comfort.

4. Repeat step three, stepping into a more and more confident you until you are overflowing with confidence. Be sure to notice how you are using your body—how you are breathing, the expression on your face, and the light in your eyes.

That is all that you need to do!

As you continue to practice the techniques in this book and listen to the accompanying CD, you will deliberately program your mind to respond to challenges and obstacles by bringing up feelings of confidence, ease, resourcefulness, and well-being.

2.

What Confidence Isn't

The Confidence Movement

When I first told people I was writing a book on confidence, the reaction I got was a bit mixed. Many people were extremely excited, and told me that they looked forward to learning more about how to access their inner resources and really go for what they wanted in their lives. But a few people said things like "Oh, great—a training manual for jerks."

> *"Be yourself; everyone else is already taken."*
> Oscar Wilde

In the seventies, psychology went through what has become known as "the confidence movement." Assertiveness classes were all the rage, and "fake it 'til you make it" became the mantra of the "me" generation.

What nobody seemed to realize at the time is that continually pretending to be something you are not just contributes to your *lack* of confidence and self-worth. After all, if you need to spend all that time pretending to be someone else you must be pretty uncomfortable about who you really are.

Unfortunately, instead of responding to that insight by seeking to become more authentic, most people stick their heads even deeper into the sand and "pretend harder." You have probably met those people who attend motivational power weekends and you can't wait to get away from them.

One client of mine was an extremely high achiever who had gradually descended into a state of depression in the months before consulting with me. When I asked him about what might be contributing to his depression, he mentioned a "harmless" habit he had fallen into of slightly exaggerating his accomplishments in every situation.

If he had made a ten-thousand-dollar profit on a business transaction, he would tell people he'd made eleven thousand. If he shot a 78 on the golf course, he would report his score as 76. Even if his actual results were phenomenal by most people's standards, he would "up the numbers" a little bit in an attempt to make himself look better.

What became obvious as we spoke was that this was in fact the source of his depression. No matter how well he did or how much he achieved, he could never do as well or achieve as much as the ideal self he was presenting to the world.

The Fear of the Average

Have you ever met one of those people who is really in your face?

Some people are overly assertive, or they can't wait to tell you how much they have or who they know, because they are "so successful." These people confuse confidence with arrogance or brashness. They confuse outer show with inner strength.

> "I still feel like I gotta prove something. There are a lot of people hoping I fail. But I like that. I need to be hated."
>
> HOWARD STERN

In fact, people who come across as arrogant usually suffer from a distinct lack of confidence at the very core of their being.

What this ultimately stems from is what psychologists call "the fear of the average," and for those people who are living in fear, trying to become more confident is really a thinly disguised form of self-attack—a desperate attempt to paper the cracks on a very delicate and easily bruised ego. And when the ego is in charge, things tend to go terribly wrong.

The ego, also known as the personality, has two primary directives:

1. To Look Good

2. To Be Right

You'll know those moments when your ego is in charge because you'll spend all of your time and energy either playing to the cameras, defending your position, or both.

Whenever I see any extremes in attitude or behavior, they appear to me as a red flag for someone's lack of inner confidence. A wacky dress sense or zany personality is often just an attempt to compensate for the fear of being ordinary.

Worse still, people who are out of touch with their natural confidence don't just try to build themselves up, they also try to bring others around them down. They use their wealth, fame, or status like weapons, asserting their moral or intellectual "superiority" over mere mortals like you or me.

Your Authentic Self

Underneath the many layers of your ego is your authentic self—the you who was there before years of unconscious programming by the world around you created the personality that the people around you are all too familiar with.

This authentic self is intrinsically valuable, completely unique, and naturally confident. Its primary directive is simple:

To be authentic in every situation.

That is why this book won't help you to create a more convincing facade to try and fool the world. Instead, it will bring you more deeply in touch with your authentic self and fill you with dynamic energy to go for what you want.

Do this exercise now:

Tapping into Your Authentic Power

Stop for a moment and really take time to vividly imagine how would your life be if you were more at ease with yourself than you are now . . .

How would your posture be?

Shift your body so you're sitting like that now. Sit the way you would be sitting if you were feeling completely confident and congruent. Feel the feeling of confidence, strength, and ease behind your eyes.

How would your voice sound? What kind of thoughts would you have about yourself and what you can achieve? What kind of things would you say to yourself?

Remember, the more you do these exercises, the faster your life will change. As you practice following my instructions fully and completely and giving each exercise your full, congruent commitment, you are naturally becoming the confident, dynamic person you really are!

3.

Your Amazing
Mind

Mind Mechanics

Your mind is like a computer—it has its own software that helps you to organize your thinking and behavior. If you have a behavior that you want to change it's just a matter of conditioning or programming. Having worked with all sorts of people with different problems over many years, I have learned that almost all problems stem from the same cause—negative programs running in the unconscious mind.

> "Those who cannot change their minds cannot change anything."
> —George Bernard Shaw

But the mind is neither positive nor negative in nature. When you think about all the amazing inventions, music, movies, poetry, architecture, and scientific achievements throughout history, all of them came from the human mind. In fact, if you look around you right now, most of what you see first began as an idea in one person's mind.

Scientists often talk about how complex the human brain is with its billions of interconnecting neurons. However, after many years of research we now understand that the mind operates on a few very simple principles. In fact, it's really quite mechanical.

Your Conscious Mind

There are only two primary ways we make sense of the world—consciously and unconsciously. Throughout this book, I will be referring to them as your conscious and unconscious mind.

Your conscious mind is the mind that you actively and deliberately think with all day long. You probably experience it as a fairly continual internal voice that you think of as "me."

But while the conscious mind certainly has its uses, it is extremely limited in what it can accomplish on its own. Studies have shown that it can only hold a handful of ideas at any one time. That's why the majority of your life is run automatically by your other mind.

Your Unconscious Mind

The unconscious mind is your larger mind. It can process millions of messages of sensory information every single second, and contains all of your wisdom, memories, and intelligence. It is the source of your creativity and, perhaps most important for our purposes here, it stores and runs all the "programs" of automatic behavior that you use to live your life.

The unconscious mind is like having an "autopilot" function in the brain that allows us to do multiple things simultaneously without having to concentrate on all of them at once. For example, when you were a child you had to concentrate consciously in order to learn to tie your shoelaces properly, using your conscious mind. But once you mastered the program, your unconscious mind could now direct your hands without your having to focus on the process consciously.

These programs ("habits") are useful because they free our conscious minds up to think about other things. Learning to drive a car involves learning lots of little habits—signaling, accelerating, braking, turning, etc.—that become habitual so that now you can just get in the car and decide where you want to go.

But as we shall see, sometimes we need to change, override, upgrade, or even completely discard our old, outdated programs.

So many of our habits are simply things we picked up by accident and never got rid of. They may not even have been helpful to us at the time. For example, many of us were told as children that we were not good enough, at least in certain areas of our lives. As adults, we still allow that old program to run our behavior, spending inordinate amounts of time worrying that we are not good enough and criticizing ourselves for not performing as well as we should have.

The good news is, all that is about to change!

The Awesome Force of Habit

The wonderful thing about our unconscious habits is that they allow us to carry out tasks and make new choices without having to use deliberate attention. In theory, we could spend most of our waking hours consciously considering all of the different

> *"We first make our habits, then our habits make us."*
> JOHN DRYDEN

alternatives available to us every single day—but we wouldn't have any time left to actually do anything about whatever it is we finally choose. In order not to waste our days considering and reconsidering those millions of attitudinal and behavioral possibilities, we've developed the capacity to make "automatic" choices instead.

For example, when we get up in the morning, we don't spend twenty minutes running through the options for breakfast. On ordinary days we just have the same thing we normally have. We usually take the same route to work, read the same newspaper, and listen to the same radio station. We cook and eat and tie our shoelaces and comb our hair in pretty much the same way, day after day after day.

We do a thousand and one daily tasks without having to think about them, simply by using the "habit force" of our unconscious mind. In this way, our largely unconscious mental programs keep our lives running smoothly.

The basic mechanism of these habits is association. Our unconscious mind remembers every time two things happen simultaneously or in close proximity to one another. After this pattern repeats itself a few times or in an emotionally significant way, the one thing gets associated to the other. So in the morning the alarm rings and we "just know" to get up and go to the bathroom. We go into the kitchen and "just know" to switch on the coffee maker. Soon, we make bigger habits out of lots of little ones all joined together.

The brain is a mass of neural pathways and every action we take creates new connections. Each time we repeat an action, that specific neural pathway is strengthened, just like a muscle that becomes bigger the more it is used. This is how a new habit is formed.

The best way to accelerate the rate at which we program a new behavior into our unconscious mind is through the imagination. The CD contained in this book will help you rehearse success over and over again in your mind, just as athletes visualize winning again and again in order to guarantee success.

While you become absorbed into a natural state of relaxation, I will program the computer—your unconscious mind—to help you become instantly, habitually, and naturally confident. The really important thing is to listen to the CD over and over again, every single day. As you practice thinking of yourself as naturally confident, you are sending signals to your unconscious mind to behave as a more naturally confident person.

And the programming has already begun . . .

4.

The Power of
Positive Self-Talk

The Hypnotist in Your Head

After watching my public appearances, people often tell me they are amazed at the powerful effect of the hypnotic suggestions I make during the show. What they don't realize is that they are making equally powerful suggestions to their unconscious mind all day long.

> "Freedom is a condition of mind, and the best way to secure it is to breed it."
>
> ELBERT HUBBARD

For example, when you are about to try something for the first time, do you tell yourself, "I bet this is going to be fun!" or do you say things to yourself like "I can't do this," "Who do you think you are?", or even "I might as well not even try—things never work out for me anyway"?

We all need our internal voice to help us navigate our way through the world. It's useful to be able to say things to ourselves like "I must remember to call Frank" or "Umm, I like the look of her" or "Get out of the way—car coming!"

However, far too often we use the power of our self-talk to limit us by talking ourselves out of doing something before we have even tried. Most people are continually giving themselves suggestions for bad feelings, inaction, and a lack of confidence, and then wonder why they feel so bad!

Imagine you had someone living in your home with you who continually pointed out everything that was wrong with you and your life in a really annoying tone of voice. How long would it take for you to want to kick that person out of your house and out of your life?

Well, your mind is the one place where you have complete dominion. And if the voice living in your head isn't supporting you, it's time to replace it with one that does. Because like it or not, the results you are getting in your life have everything to do with what that voice keeps telling you.

What Are You Suggesting?

As an experiment, listen to your internal voice over the course of today and notice the number of negative suggestions you are giving yourself. You may even want to write them down so that you can get them out of your head and see them for what they are.

In fact, for the next week, whenever you catch yourself saying something negative about yourself in your mind I want you to do this:

STOP IT!

Now let me be clear—I'm not suggesting that you go around pretending that you're perfect. I'm just saying that when you speak to yourself in a more positive manner, you will get more positive results.

What you feed gets stronger, and as you stop criticizing yourself and begin cheering yourself on instead, you will not only begin feeling better, you will be growing stronger and more naturally confident each day.

Beyond Affirmations

Many self-help books preach the gospel of "affirmations"—positive statements about yourself that are

> "Good words are worth much and cost little."
> GEORGE HERBERT

meant to be repeated out loud hundreds of times each day in order to program your mind to be more positive.

But saying something out loud has nowhere near the same impact on your feelings and behaviors as hearing the same things inside your mind. And if you're telling yourself wonderful things on the outside while your internal voice is telling you it's all bullshit, your internal voice's suggestions will win every time.

The exercise on the following page will help you to use the power of your internal voice to increase your levels of confidence. After you have practiced this technique several times throughout the day today, continue to use it as often as you can for the next few weeks until it becomes a habit.

Remember, by practicing these exercises in conjunction with the CD I have specially recorded for this book, you and I will be instructing your unconscious mind to automatically reprogram yourself to be naturally confident in every situation.

Programming Your Mind for Confidence and Success

Read through the exercise before you do it for the first time . . .

1. Locate your internal voice. Just ask yourself "Where is my internal voice?" and point to the location where you hear the words.

2. Now, I would like you to imagine how your voice sounds if it is totally confident. Is it louder or softer than usual? Is it clearer and easier to hear? Stronger or weaker? Do you speak faster or more slowly?

   However your voice sounds when you are really positive and confident, put that voice in the same location where your old internal voice was located.

3. Take a few moments to think of some of the negative suggestions you have habitually given yourself in the past, things like:

   "I'm not very confident."
   "I am terrible at giving presentations."
   "I will never find someone to fall in love with me."

4. For each statement, come up with its positive opposite.

   "I'm a naturally confident person."
   "I give excellent presentations."
   "I am extremely loveable."

5. Finally, I want you to repeat the new, positive suggestion to yourself in your new confident internal voice.

It feels totally different when you talk to yourself like that, doesn't it?

Remember, what you practice you become. Just keep practicing talking to yourself in a positive way until the positive suggestions override the negative, and be sure to reinforce your self-programming with the accompanying CD!

5.

The Movies in Your Mind

A Natural Ability

Have you ever heard someone say, "I just can't see myself doing that"?

This phrase more than any other acts as a command to your unconscious mind, preventing you from accessing your innermost confident resources.

> "I never hit a shot, not even in practice, without having a very sharp in-focus picture of it in my head."
>
> JACK NICKLAUS

Yet in my experience, *everybody* has the ability to visualize. To prove this to yourself, answer the following questions:

1. **What color is your front door?**

2. **Which side is the handle on?**

In order to answer either of these questions, you had to go into your imagination and make a picture. These pictures will not be "photo quality"—and that's a good thing. We need to be able to see the difference between what's real and what's imaginary.

Let's try an experiment . . .

I'd like you to remember a time you felt good. Return to it as though you are back there right now. See what you saw, hear what you heard and feel how good you felt. Go through the memory a couple of times, remembering new details each time . . .

The reason you are probably feeling pretty good right now is simple:

> **The human nervous system cannot tell the difference between a real and a vividly imagined experience.**

When we think about happy memories, we re-create the happy feeling associated with them. When we think about times in the past where we felt bad, we recreate those feelings as well.

But just as with your internal voice, it's not just what we choose to picture in our minds but the *way* we do it that's important.

For example . . .

Remember that happy memory again, but this time make the image larger than life size. Make it even bigger, brighter and more colorful. Do it now!

Generally speaking images that are bigger, brighter, and more colorful have greater emotional intensity than those that are smaller, duller, and dimmer.

You can use the same technique to take the emotion out of a negative memory . . .

Think of a mildly unpleasant experience from your past. Float out of yourself so that you can see the back of your head as you push the picture of the memory off into the distance. When it's at least twenty feet away, shrink the image down and drain the color out until it's black and white. As you see whatever it was that happened to that other you "over there," you can fade it completely out until it is no more than a dim and distant part of your past . . .

What's Playing Between Your Ears?

All champion athletes use visualization as a deliberate training tool, imagining winning an event over and over again in their mind until their mind and body know exactly what it is they want to do.

As you become more aware of your internal world, you will realize that you too are unconsciously making little movies in your mind all day long. These "mind movies" affect your feelings and, in turn, determine your levels of confidence and subsequent behavior.

For example, if you are due to give a presentation and all you do is make movies in your imagination of you looking nervous and forgetting what you are going to say, then you will create feelings of fear and discomfort in yourself that will make you dread giving the presentation.

> "The human race is governed by its imagination."
>
> NAPOLEON

If, on the other hand, you make a movie in your mind of a friendly group of people who are fascinated by what you have to say and you imagine the words flowing easily as you engage your audience fully and completely, then you are going to feel much more confident about giving the presentation.

There are many applications of this principle, and much scientific evidence to back it up. New research into "mental architecture" has shown that consistent patterns of thought and behavior actually lead to physical changes in the shape of the brain, suggesting that there is a genuine physiological basis for repetition and "perfect practice" leading to success in any endeavor.

When the famous football coach Vince Lombardi took over the Green Bay Packers, the first thing he did was to insist that from that moment on, the only highlight films the team were allowed to watch were of their own most successful games, and within those games, only the most successful, effectively run plays.

His philosophy was simple—what you practice, you become. The Green Bay Packers went on to win the first two Super Bowls, and to become one of the greatest teams in American football history.

Let's do a powerful visualization exercise that will increase your confidence right now:

Success Highlight Films

Read through the exercise before you do it for the first time . . .

1. I'd like you to imagine right now that you are watching a movie about a future, more successful you. Notice every detail of how that future you looks—the expression on your face, the way you are holding your body, and the light in your eyes.

2. As the movie plays out on the screen in front of you, you will see many moments of success from your past and others that have not yet happened. Sit back and enjoy the show!

3. When you're ready, I'd like you to float out of your seat and into that successful you up on the screen. See through their eyes, hear through their ears and feel the feelings of your successful self. Make the colors brighter, the sounds louder and the feelings stronger.

4. Notice where that feeling of success is strongest in your body and give it a color. Now move that color up to the top of your head and down to the tip of your toes, doubling the brightness and doubling it again.

5. Float back into your present moment self, being sure to keep as much of the feeling of natural confidence and success as feels truly wonderful.

You can watch your success highlight films as often as you like, but especially as part of the Five Minute Daily Confidence Workout, which you will be learning in chapter 14. Each time you run it, you can make any changes that occur to you to "increase the juice" of good feelings it gives you.

If it helps, you can imagine putting in and taking out an appropriately labeled DVD before and after each showing. No matter how well you visualize, you may find it easier if you write your "film" out as a story and read it out loud before closing your eyes and imagining it fully!

Here are a few more tricks real movie makers use to add "oomph" to their movies . . .

1. **Add a good soundtrack. Many athletes get themselves into an optimal performance state by listening to an uplifting, energizing piece of music before a competition. The actor Johnny Depp actually listens to music while filming a scene to get himself "in the mood."**

2. **Use bright colors and big, bold, moving images—there's a reason it's more fun to see an action movie on a huge screen than on a twelve-inch black and white TV!**

As you become more practiced at visualizing yourself succeeding rather than failing, your feelings of confidence and motivation will increase. As a result, your behavior will begin to change. Soon you will have reprogrammed yourself to go for what you want with ease and comfort—a natural sense of confidence.

6.

Use Your Body to Change Your Life

The Posture of Champions

Your mind and body are intimately linked in what is known as a "cybernetic loop." That means that whatever you think will affect the way your body feels, and the way you use your body will affect the thoughts in your head. Put simply, the one is always affecting the other.

> "Nothing is more revealing than movement."
> MARTHA GRAHAM

Think about someone you know who is depressed. You will notice that their body posture is hardly ever upright. They tend to slouch and their movements are slow.

Now contrast that with champion sports people, business leaders, and the most successful figures in show business. Notice what their postures have in common. Most of the time you'll see them "standing tall," but in a relaxed way. They move their bodies in bold, confident ways.

Try this experiment:

Imagine a silver cord running up your spine and out through the top of your head. Now imagine that cord is gently pulling up on the back of your head, making your body more and more upright.

For the next few days, practice sitting and moving in this new way. By making this one simple change in the way you carry yourself, you will send a whole new set of messages to yourself and the world about how naturally confident you really are. Soon, you will have reset the muscle memory and this new confident posture will become your predominant habit.

One Point of Power

Many years ago I was at a health exhibition when I walked past a rather small, nerdy-looking man wearing a martial arts outfit. My friend and I stopped and began having a conversation with him about aikido. He explained that aikido is a defensive martial art where the main focus is upon using your opponent's energy against him while staying centered in yourself.

To our delight, he agreed to give us a demonstration. He asked me to gently push him, and as he was more than a foot shorter than me I had no problem knocking him off balance.

Then he smiled and said, "Now push me again." I did as he asked but something had changed—he didn't move at all. He told me to push harder, so I pushed as hard as I could but it felt like he was made of concrete.

> "The key to good technique is to keep your hands, feet, and hips straight and centered. If you are centered, you can move freely. The physical center is your belly; if your mind is set there as well, you are assured of victory in any endeavor."
>
> MORIHEI UESHIBA, FOUNDER OF AIKIDO

He smiled again and said, "Ask your friend to help you." My burly friend and I were now both putting our backs into it but to no avail. Someone even stopped by to ask him a question, which he calmly answered as we groaned and pushed in vain against him.

When we finally gave up, I asked him how in the hell he had just done that. He explained that when we move our attention to the very center of our body, we become physically and psychologically stronger.

He then asked me to think about something or someone that I found stressful—my boss at the time came instantly to mind! Then he told me to forget about the room and people around and to "put my brain in my tummy." I thought what the hell, and gave it a try, moving my attention directly into my stomach. He pushed hard on my shoulder but I could barely feel it. I not only felt physically stronger, I felt calmer. When he asked me to once again think about my boss, I noticed that I no longer felt stressed—I felt strong.

Here is the very same exercise for you to learn and master. You can use it to prepare for a potentially difficult situation or as an "in the moment" tool to center your mind and body for confident success . . .

One Point

Read through the exercise before you do it for the first time . . .

A quick note: It can be useful to do this for the first time with the assistance of another person, but if you don't have anyone to do it with, you can always do it for yourself.

1. Stand up and put your attention on your "One Point"—about an inch below your navel and roughly halfway between your navel and your spine. This point is known in Japanese as *hara* and in Chinese as *tan tien,* and is believed to be both the physical center of your body and the central storage point for your *ki, chi,* or life force. If it helps, place one hand over that area of your stomach—I find for me that if I line my thumb up across my navel, that works well for me. You may also like to visualize a ball of energy radiating from that spot.

2. Now think about a situation coming up in your life that you are worried or upset about. (This is not the time for major phobias—start with something relatively minor!) If you have someone working with you, have them push you gently on the shoulder. You will find you are very easily pushed off balance.

3. Continue thinking about that difficult situation. Give your discomfort level a score from 1 (at peace) to 10 (aaaargh!).

4. Now bring your attention back to "One Point." Place your hand over that area of your stomach

to help guide your mind. If you have someone working with you, have them once again push you gently on the shoulder. You will know you are at "One Point" when it is very difficult for them to push you off balance.

5. Finally, holding "One Point" attention, think about the situation you were upset or worried about and notice the discomfort drain away from 10 (or wherever it was on the scale) down to 1. Again, if someone is working with you they can monitor your attention by pushing gently against your shoulder as you do this to make sure you are holding "One Point."

6. When you no longer feel discomfort thinking about the situation, you can use your "One Point" attention to mentally rehearse performing at your best. When you are actually in the situation, you can hold "One Point" as you perform to ensure you will stay centered and peaceful throughout.

7.

Emotional Intelligence

Why Do We Feel
What We Feel?

Recent scientific research has shown that people's emotional baseline is set within the first few years of life. Unless they experience a major life change, most people will never feel significantly higher or lower than they have learned to be during that time.

> "We have tamed the
> beasts and schooled
> the lightning . . .
> but we have still to
> tame ourselves."
>
> H. G. WELLS

By doing the exercises in this book and listening to the CD, you are raising your emotional baseline. You will still be able to feel a full, dynamic range of emotions, but your highs will be higher and your lows will be higher as well.

People often think that because I teach and practice these tools on a daily basis, I must never feel bad or uncomfortable. While I do choose to feel good in most situations, I always take the time to feel my feelings and listen to any messages they may have for me.

Your emotions are not just sensations that float around your body, causing you to feel better or worse at random. They are actually an important part of your intelligence. Emotions are your unconscious mind's way of telling you that there is something going on in your life you need to pay closer attention to.

For many centuries, Western cultures have placed a high value on suppressing and ignoring emotional reactions. This is not only a bad idea—it's a potentially dangerous one.

Imagine if you asked someone to wake you up in the morning because you had important things to do. They tried whispering your name, gently nudging you, and even shouting. Eventually, they would have to tip you out of bed or pour a bucket of ice-cold water on you just to get a response.

This kind of rude awakening happens to many people who have consistently ignored their emotional messages over time, burying themselves in work, drink, food, or drugs rather than dealing with uncomfortable feelings as they arise. The more they ignore their feelings, the more intense the feelings get, until incidents of depression, anger, violence, and illness lead to problems that can no longer be ignored.

Fortunately, this is now beginning to change. With the advent of more and more books and courses teaching about "emotional intelligence," both science and society are beginning to recognize the importance of being aware of and in touch with our innermost feelings.

Increasing Your EQ

Meeting and understanding our uncomfortable feelings is how we learn and grow as people. Emotions are, if you like, our sixth sense—they change and evolve over time because both we and our lives change as time passes.

> "The happiness of the human race in this world does not consist in our being devoid of passions, but in our learning to command them."
>
> ANONYMOUS

However, it's important to be able to tell the difference between feelings that arise as unconscious reactions to the pictures and sounds in your head and the deeper emotions that carry important messages that you can learn from.

Here is the test:

When you are feeling an uncomfortable emotion, change what you are saying to yourself in your head, the pictures you are making in your mind, and the way you are using your body. If the same emotion keeps coming back, it may have an important message for you from your unconscious mind.

For example, if you visualize giving a presentation perfectly and begin to feel much better, you were worrying unnecessarily. If even after imagining yourself doing it perfectly, your feeling of discomfort doesn't change, you need to ask yourself, "What do I need to pay attention to here? What is the message that you have for me?"

The more you establish a sense of connection with your emotions, the more in control of your life you feel and the more quickly you will be able to pick up and act on the messages they are sending you. In this way, you are becoming more and more emotionally intelligent.

Learning from Our Emotions

One of the things I've noticed that really marks a significant turning point for people is the moment when they stop repressing or distracting their feelings and begin instead to listen for the message underlying them.

> "There can be no knowledge without emotion."
> ARNOLD BENNETT

Here are some of the most common emotional messages we receive on an almost daily basis, and some insight into what they usually mean:

Anger is usually a sign that one of our rules or boundaries has been violated, either by ourselves or by someone else. The message is to either take action for what we believe is right or, in some cases, to accept the things we cannot change.

Fear is really just a warning that something bad *could* happen, so you'd better be prepared. If you feel that you are fully prepared, or if you are experiencing fear in a situation where you normally feel comfortable, it could be a genuine warning of physical danger.

Frustration arises when you're not achieving the level of results you believe you should in the timeframe you believe you should achieve them. The message is usually to take some time to reflect on your level of commitment to the goal and/or your strategy for achieving it. Once you have done so, you can either recommit, drop the goal, or change your strategy.

Guilt tends to come about whenever you are not living up to one of your own standards of conduct. Guilt's message is very simple—don't do it again and do what needs to be done to put it right!

Sadness is the result of feeling that something is missing from our lives, either because we've lost it or we've lost touch with it. The underlying message is both to appreciate what you've lost and to be grateful for what you still have. In some cases, the message may be to fight to get it back, as in the case of a "lost love" or an abandoned dream.

If you can't find what you're feeling on the list above or if what's written there doesn't fit for you, here's an exercise that will help you in listening to and hearing the important messages your emotions want to bring you . . .

Emotional Wisdom

Read through the exercise before you do it for the first time . . .

1. Clarify the emotion that you are finding uncomfortable. Don't be distracted by thinking about WHY you are feeling it—just focus on the feeling itself. Where in your body do you feel it? Are there certain situations, times, places, or people with whom it tends to arise?

2. Next, ask yourself what the feeling is about—what message does it have for you? If you're not sure, it's okay to guess—whatever you guess will inevitably come directly from your intuitive self.

3. Whatever the message, let your unconscious mind know you've received it. If there is any action to be taken, promise yourself you will take it as soon as possible—ideally within the next twenty-four hours.

4. You'll know you've correctly identified the emotion and its message when the uncomfortable feeling begins to dissolve into the background and your natural, confident sense of ease and well-being returns to the fore.

8.

Self-Belief

Isn't "Believing in Myself" Just a Cliché?

Do you believe in yourself? Do you think it matters?

In one of the most detailed studies ever conducted into the effects of self-belief on performance, the psychologist Albert Bandura discovered that a person's genuine beliefs about their capabilities can be a more accurate predictor of their future levels of performance than any actual results they had produced in the past.

> *"It's lack of faith that makes people afraid of meeting challenges, and I believe in myself."*
>
> MUHAMMAD ALI

In other words, the way you think about yourself in relationship to the challenges you are currently facing in your life will have a profound impact on your ability to succeed.

The mechanism by which it works is called "the self-fulfilling prophecy."

The Power of Prophecy

You have probably heard of the notion of self-fulfilling prophecies before. For example, if someone believes that they are unattractive and that no one they actually like could ever possibly be interested in them, how would you expect them to behave?

Will they approach someone they are attracted to?

If they do, will they use their body and mind in a confident way?

Are they likely to be focused on making the other person feel comfortable and good about themselves while they are with them?

When someone shows interest in them are they likely to respond to it or dismiss it?

Because they believe the way that they do, they don't take the actions that could lead to disproving the belief. Therefore, they bring about the very condition that they wish weren't so, thereby "proving" their belief to be true.

Eventually, they will simply conclude that there is no point in even trying, and so the prophecy is fulfilled.

Fortunately, we can use the same power for self-fulfilling prophecy to build our confidence and massively increase the likelihood of our success.

Cognitive Dissonance

In 1955, a charismatic middle-aged woman named Marion Keech began claiming she was receiving messages from the planet "Clarion." Eventually, these messages revealed to her that a great flood would come and destroy the world on December 21, but that flying saucers would be coming to rescue her and her faithful followers.

> *"I knew I was a winner back in the late sixties. I knew I was destined for great things. People will say that kind of thinking is totally immodest. I agree. Modesty is not a word that applies to me in any way—I hope it never will."*
>
> ARNOLD SCHWARZENEGGER

In preparation for the historic day, many of her devotees resigned from their jobs, sold their possessions, and gave away their money (after all, they wouldn't be needing Christmas presents that year).

On the morning of December 21, Mrs. Keech and her followers assembled on a mountaintop to await their deliverance. But to everyone's surprise, the flying saucers never came. Fortunately, neither did the great flood.

Now, you might think that having given up everything, her followers would be a tad disappointed, but when Marion Keech reported that she had received a new message that the world had been spared from the apocalypse because of the "faith of her group and the light they had spread upon the Earth," the group celebrated.

Instead of slinking home to prepare for a present-less Christmas in an empty house with smug "I told you so" relatives, they contacted everyone they could in the media to explain what a wonderful event had occurred.

Why would seemingly sane people act in such a seemingly insane way?

Because one of the mind's primary functions is to prove itself right. According to social psychologist Leon Festinger, the state of trying to hold two inconsistent ideas, beliefs, or opinions (known as "cognitive dissonance") is so uncomfortable that people will unconsciously seek to reduce the conflict by changing one or both of these ideas so that they "fit together" better.

In other words, your mind wants to stay consistent with whatever you have previously said or demonstrated you believe to be true. You can't become rich if you're constantly criticizing rich people— your mind won't stand for it. Similarly, you can't sit around resenting confident, successful people and be surprised that your mind doesn't want you to join them.

Is there a part of you that really wants to be more confident and successful but another part that's not so sure? If that's the case you'll probably find that sometimes you self-sabotage—you start to be successful and suddenly you do something to stop yourself. It's a bit like driving down the street with one foot on the accelerator and the other on the brake.

Here is a simple exercise you can use to resolve that creative tension and increase your self-belief in any situation . . .

As you practice this technique, you will find it becomes easier and easier to resolve every internal conflict in this way. And when all parts of yourself are aligned and moving in the same direction, you will have become focused like a laser beam on whatever you decide to do!

Creating Integrated Self-Belief

Read through the exercise before you do it for the first time . . .

1. Identify the two conflicting beliefs or positions within your mind.

   For example, part of you might want to be more confident, part of you might want to stay fearful because it believes that will keep you safe.

2. Place your hands out in front of you, palms up. Imagine the confident part in your dominant hand, the fearful part in your non-dominant hand.

3. Ask each part in turn what its positive intention for you is in wanting what it wants. Continue asking until you really recognize that at some level they both want the same thing. Even if it feels like you are just making it up, going through this process will create dramatic changes in your levels of confidence and self-belief.

   Example:

   Confidence ➤ More resourceful ➤ Perform Better ➤ SUCCESS!

   Fear ➤ More cautious ➤ Perform Better ➤ SUCCESS!

4. Imagine a new "super part" in between your hands with the combined resources of both your confidence and your fear. ➤

5. Moving only as quickly as you can, bring your hands together until the two separate parts become one with the super part.

6. Bring your hands in to your chest and take the new integrated image inside you.

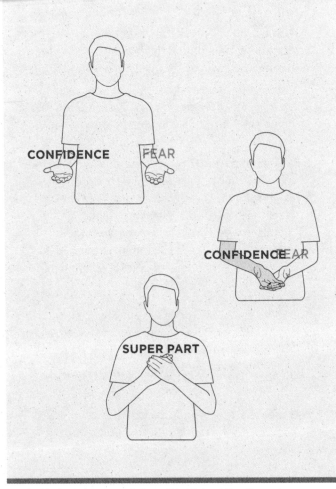

Used with the written permission of Dr. Richard Bandler

9.

You Really Can Do Anything!

Learning from the Success of Others

Have you ever looked at someone who was particularly good at something and wished you could do that too?

Confidence, optimism, security, creativity, persuasiveness, being a great golfer or salesperson are simply skills to be learned and mastered, and any skills that anyone else has mastered you can learn too.

> "The best teachers of humanity are the lives of great men."
> CHARLES H. FOWLER

Even though you might think that some people are just wiser, more talented or luckier than you, whatever it is they do so well, they do by running a particular sequence of thoughts and behaviors that have been practiced until they became habitual and automatic "success programs."

Andre Agassi's programming to become a great tennis player began when his father hung a mobile made out of tennis balls over his crib. Tiger Woods was hitting golf balls at an age when most children are still learning to walk.

The point is, babies are not born persuasive, creative, or great tennis players—they learn how to do it through a simple two-step process:

1. Copying or "modeling" how others do it.

2. Repeatedly practicing the new skill (mentally and physically) until it becomes habit.

As a child you watched how your parents walked and then you tried to copy it. Of course you fell over quite a few times before you eventually found your balance, but essentially you were just emulating what Mom and Dad did and practicing until you could do it for yourself.

If you learned to drive, you did it after years of watching how other people did it and building up a model in your mind. Then you practiced each element of the driving process until you mastered it for yourself.

What can radically accelerate the process is learning to use it deliberately and supplementing physical practice with the amazing power of your mind.

Modeling What Works

Whenever I want to learn and understand how someone does what they do, I begin by watching examples of the person I want to model doing whatever it is that I want to learn. I then practice "stepping in" to their physiology and using my body in the same way as they use theirs until the new behaviors feel natural to me.

> "Example has more followers than reason."
> JOHN CHRISTIAN BOVEE

By copying the physiology of someone who is truly confident, you will begin to develop the same confident mindsets. Remember the mind and body are intimately linked, so if you operate your body the same way as someone else you will start to have the same kinds of thoughts.

For example, when I first started working on television, I got a stack of videos of people I thought were really confident, natural, and personable on TV. These were qualities I admired in all kinds of different personalities.

I sat and watched the videos, then I relaxed, closed my eyes, and replayed the images in my mind of each of my role models in action, and one by one imagined stepping into their bodies, standing the way they stood, moving the way they moved, speaking in the same tone and in the same rhythm they spoke.

It was amazing—I began to feel totally different. My body was filled with a sort of "relaxed alertness," and the whole thing just seemed so much easier once I began looking at the world from the perspective of these successful TV performers.

I repeated the process again and again, programming my mind to encode the learning deep into my body memory. After only a short time, I was able to feel relaxed and confident on camera all by myself.

Let's do it now . . .

The Possibility Generator

Read through the exercise before you do it for the first time . . .

1. Think of someone whose confidence and charisma you wish to emulate.

2. Think of a time when they exhibited the skill you wish to learn.

3. Now, run through that memory of your role model performing that particular skill. Do this several times; if it helps, do it once in slow motion.

4. Now, go over to your role model and float into their body, and synchronize with their posture. See through their eyes, hear through their ears, and feel how confident they feel.

5. Now run through the memory of them performing the skill from the inside and get the general sense of your role model's experience.

6. Do this several times, until you have a strong sense of what it's like to be your role model.

By standing, breathing, smiling, talking, and moving the way your role model does, you'll begin to develop the same quality of thoughts and internal states as they do. You will begin to transform your experience of being alive.

But choose your role models carefully—this process really works!

10.

The 5-Minute Daily Confidence Workout

Conditioning Yourself for Success

A number of years ago, I turned on the TV to watch a program on the BBC called *How to Be Happy*.

> *"Everything is practice."*
>
> PELÉ

The idea behind the show was that Dr. Robert Holden, often referred to as "the happiness psychologist," would take three clinically depressed people and see if he could make them happier over a relatively short period of time.

Each of the participants in the show had participated in a university study to explore the amount of activity they were currently experiencing in the left prefrontal lobe of their brain, a reliable indicator of exactly how much happiness they were experiencing in their daily lives. Over the course of the next few months, the scientists would then be able to accurately measure if these people became tangibly happier.

When I saw the deadpan expressions on the people who had been chosen, I leaned forward toward the screen and thought to myself, "I can't wait to see him make these miserable people happy." On the TV show, Dr. Holden simply got them to do three things:

1. *Get physical exercise*

It has been conclusively proven that physical exercise is a powerful, natural antidote to depression. It does this by using up the adrenaline and other chemicals released into our bloodstream by stress and by relieving the tension in our muscles. In addition, regular physical exercise releases the body's natural opiates, giving you a warm, comfortable, relaxed feeling for hours afterward. Over time, these positive feelings become the new default setting for how wonderful your body can feel.

2. *Laugh for twenty minutes every day*

Laughter, even if initially it is forced and artificial, has been proven to lift our spirits and improve our overall mood and well-being. As with physical exercise, it produces endorphins to make the body feel good. Even just smiling releases serotonin (a happy neurotransmitter) into the bloodstream and acts as a powerful antidepressant.

3. *Force themselves to have positive thoughts*

Each of the participants in the study placed colored stickers all around their home and work environments. Every time they saw one, they had to think of something that made them feel good. This strengthened the neural pathways in their brains associated with pleasure and re-enforced the happy chemicals in their bodies.

Within the first month, each of these new behaviors had become automatic and habitual. At the end of the study, the participants returned to the university to once again have their brain activity measured. The results were so astounding that one of the scientists demanded to have the equipment checked.

All three participants had changed from being clinically measured as "depressive" to being measured as "extreme optimists"—they had moved from one end of the scale to the other!

They had literally rewired their neurology to become happier. When they spoke about their experiences toward the end of the show, it was obvious their personalities had changed for the better. They not only seemed happier, they looked younger.

Since that time, Dr. Holden and I have worked together on several occasions. Recently, he said to me that using the mind-programming techniques I have shared with you so far in this book, the dramatic changes from his program could have happened even faster.

I have incorporated the same elements of simple daily action and positive re-enforcement into this program. As you practice the techniques in this book and use the CD, you too will change yourself so you are hard-wired to respond to every situation with more confidence and motivation than ever before.

It's amazing that taking just a few minutes each day can produce such a profound lasting change in your life.

The 5-Minute Daily Confidence Workout

The golden rule throughout this book is "what you practice, you become." And there are only four things you need to practice to become a naturally confident person.

1. Talk to yourself in a confident way

2. Make big, bold positive pictures in your mind

3. Use your body as if you were already confident

4. Take at least one risk every single day

The more you practice doing these four things, the more naturally confident you will become. Soon, you will find yourself automatically responding to new situations with states of confidence instead of fear, with self-belief instead of doubt.

I have developed this 5-Minute Daily Confidence Workout to assist you in easily developing the confidence habit. Used in conjunction with the CD, it will transform your entire life. All you need is a bit of a paper to write on, a mirror, and 5 of the 1,440 minutes we are given to play with each and every day.

Minute One:
Success Highlight Films

Take a minute to run through the Success Highlight Film exercise you first practiced in chapter five. You can use the exercise to think about any success you have experienced in the past or look forward to experiencing in the future. Remember to juice up your memories by using bright colors and big, bold, moving images!

Minute Two:
The Mirror

1. Stand in front of a mirror and close your eyes.
2. Think about someone who loves you and imagine viewing yourself through their eyes.
3. When you are ready, open your eyes and look into the mirror. Allow yourself to really see yourself through the eyes of someone who totally loves you.

Minute Three:
Compliment Yourself

Still looking in the mirror, use your confident internal voice to compliment yourself over and over again for a full minute. If you find this difficult, it is even more important for you. Remember, you are raising your vibration so that you will attract more of what you want into your life.

Minute Four:
Push the Confidence Switch

1. Remember a time when you felt really, really confident. Fully return to it now—see what you saw, hear what you heard, and feel how good you felt. (If you can't remember a time, imagine how much better your life would be if you were totally confident—if you had all the power, strength, and self-belief you could ever need!)

2. As you keep going through this memory, make the colors brighter and richer, the sounds louder, and the feelings stronger.

3. As you feel these good feelings, squeeze the thumb and middle finger of either hand together.

4. Still holding your thumb and finger together, think about a situation coming up in the next twenty-four hours during which you want to feel more confident. Imagine things going perfectly, going exactly the way you want them to go. See what you'll see, hear what you'll hear, and feel how good it feels!

Minute Five:
Confidence in Action

1. Take a minute to write down any inspired actions that came up for you as you went through this workout.

2. Choose at least one of them that feels like a little bit of a risk to take in the next twenty-four hours!

Each time you take yourself through the 5-Minute Daily Confidence Workout, your self-belief and sense of inner comfort will increase. Unlike working out at a gym, there is no recovery time needed between workouts. The more you do each exercise, the faster your confidence will grow!

Motivate Yourself for Success

11.

What Motivates You?

A Visit to the Future

Up until now, we have been focusing primarily on the *state* of confidence—that feeling in your body of being comfortable, powerful, and at ease. But feeling confident is only half of the recipe for success. If all you did was sit around all day feeling confident, your life would not change for the better. In order to truly make a difference in your life, you need to take consistent daily action.

> "Motivation is what gets you started. Habit is what keeps you going."
> JIM RYUN

Do this now . . .

Imagine it is now the future, a few years before the end of your life. You never took action to create the changes you want in your life. How do you feel? What does it inspire you to do or not do now?

Whatever your experience of that was, come fully back into the present . . .

Now, I'd like you to imagine you're way off into the future again, near the end of your life. But in this future, you've taken action every single day to make your life the way you want it. How is this future different? How do you feel? What does living in this way inspire you to do or not do now?

We all have things we are motivated to move toward and other things we are motivated to move away from. Whichever combination of the two inspires you to take action is your own personal key to motivation!

Instant Motivation

We all have the seeds of motivation within us. For example, if your house was on fire, would you sit around on the sofa until *American Idol* had ended before calling the fire department and getting yourself and your loved ones out of there? If you

> "What we see depends mainly on what we look for."
> SIR JOHN LUBBOCK

won the lottery, would you procrastinate for a few weeks before you eventually got around to collecting your millions?

In each of these examples, the "on/off switch" for your motivation was something outside yourself. But what if you were able to switch on your motivation all by yourself, without waiting for some external event to trigger you into action?

You only have to look at the Internet to realize that people can attach feelings of pleasure to pretty much anything (so I'm told). So imagine what would happen if you deliberately attached feelings of powerful motivation to whatever it is you most want to do?

The talk show host Montel Williams, a former sergeant in the U.S. Marines, asked me to demonstrate this principle on his show. They found a guy who was completely unmotivated to do any cleaning up around the house. I went to his home with a camera crew at eleven a.m. and we found him lying on the couch drinking a bottle of beer.

When I asked him what already motivated him, he couldn't think of anything. Noticing the pool cues against the wall, I asked him if he liked to play pool. His entire posture changed. His face lit up and he began talking excitedly about how much he loved playing pool for money.

I had him vividly remember one of his most exciting matches and create a "switch" for instant motivation, just like the confidence switch you learned to create in section one. To make the switch more powerful, I asked him to think about his most exciting sexual experience and to add that feeling to the switch. Finally, I asked him to remember a time when he thought to himself, "What the hell—I'm just going to do this!" and we added those feelings to the switch as well. By this time, he was ready to explode with motivation!

All that remained was to link that feeling of incredible excitement and pleasurable anticipation to doing the housework. I had him push the switch and think about the housework, push the switch and think about the housework, push the switch and think about the housework until we actually had to hold him back from getting started until we could get the cameras into position.

A few minutes later he was happily ironing away in his living room with a dishrack full of newly cleaned dishes gleaming in the kitchen next door. The only problem was that he had attached so much good feeling to using the vacuum cleaner that he kept turning the switch on and off to deliver himself more and more pleasure. Less than an hour after we'd arrived to find him slobbed out on his sofa, we had to leave the room so he could have some "alone time" with his newly beloved vacuum cleaner!

What would you love to be really motivated to do?

The following exercise will give you the power to unleash your motivation in any situation . . .

The Motivation Switch

Read through the exercise before you do it for the first time . . .

1. Think about something you would love to be really motivated to do.

2. Now, remember a time when you felt really, really motivated in the past—a time when you took positive action and made a difference in your life. Fully return to it now—see what you saw, hear what you heard, and feel how good you felt. If you can't remember a time, what happens when you think about how much better your life would be if you were totally motivated to take action now? Imagine how good you would feel if you had all the confidence, power, tenacity, and determination you could ever need!

3. As you keep going through this memory, make the colors brighter, the sounds richer, and the feelings stronger. Tell yourself to "Go for it!" in your most confident inner voice!

4. While you are feeling these good feelings, squeeze the thumb and middle finger of either hand together. From now on, each time you squeeze your thumb and middle finger together, you will begin to relive these good feelings.

5. Repeat steps 1–4 several times, adding in new positive experiences of motivation each time until just squeezing your thumb and middle

finger together brings those good feelings back up to the top and has you raring to go.

6. Still holding your thumb and finger together, think about that situation in which you want to feel more motivated. Imagine things going perfectly, exactly the way you want them to be. See what you'll see, hear what you'll hear, and feel how good it feels to get into action and make things happen!

Just by taking the time to complete this exercise, you have set into motion the awesome power of momentum in your life. Whatever you set your mind on doing will be easier to achieve than ever before, because you have now put yourself in charge of your own motivation.

So . . . what are you going to do with the rest of your life?

12.

Goals, Goals, Goals!

The Power of a Goal

Everything I have ever achieved in my life is the result of planning. That doesn't mean that nothing spontaneous ever happens in my life—it means that I am very clear at all times about the direction in which I am headed.

> *"Man is a goal-seeking animal. His life only has meaning if he is reaching out and striving for his goals."*
>
> ARISTOTLE

Research studies consistently show that having goals makes a significant difference in creating success, and the biographies of high achievers throughout history bear out the research. So if you want to achieve anything worthwhile you absolutely have to have goals—but how you design your goals can make all the difference in the world.

Size Really Does Matter

Your goals have to be big enough to get you out of bed—to make you feel motivated even before you push the switch. Just being "a little more efficient at work," or "losing five pounds" is rarely a big enough target to aim at. You need BIG goals—goals that will ignite your passion and get you off your duff and into action. Then all the things that you do in your daily life become easier. As Donald Trump has said, "You have 50,000 thoughts a day—you might as well make them big ones!"

Years ago I used to take forever to wake up in the morning and get going. I had tried setting goals about "getting up a bit earlier," or "waking up with energy," but nothing worked. Then one day I sat down and began creating BIG goals for myself—goals like having my own TV show, creating a business empire, and making a massive positive difference to the world. At first I didn't really notice the difference—but everyone around me did.

For example, I remember leaping out of bed at five a.m. one morning to travel to the north of England for an appearance on the *Richard and Judy* TV show. My girlfriend asked me why I was so energized. When I thought about it, I realized that I now saw each small action I took as part of the big picture of building my brand. With my BIG goal in mind, getting out of bed in the morning simply wasn't a problem anymore.

Who Cares What You Don't Want?

When I was a child, my mother repeatedly told my brother and me, "Don't smoke cigarettes." Before she began talking about it, the thought hadn't even entered my mind—but after repeated exposure to the power of her suggestion, I became so curious that before long I was standing behind the bicycle shed coughing my guts up.

That story came to mind a few years ago when I was working with a champion golfer who had begun consistently hitting balls into the bunkers. When I went with him to the course and watched him play, I was amazed that he not only consistently hit the ball into the bunker, but perfectly into the middle of the sand. After asking him a few questions, it became apparent what he was doing.

Every time he was setting up for a shot, he would make a picture in his mind of the ball going in the bunker, put a red X through the picture and tell himself, "I must not *hit it in the bunker!*" In other words, he was programming his mind to do exactly what he didn't want.

On the very next hole, I asked the golfer to think about NOT hitting it in the hole. Although he looked at me as if I was nuts, he did what I told him to do. His very next shot landed about 3 feet from the hole.

The reason this worked so well is that in order to "not do" something, you first have to think about doing it. For example, try not to think about elephants right now—go on—no elephants.

This is also why it's so important that as you work on creating your BIG goals, you focus exclusively on what it is that you DO want. Rehearse achieving it in your mind. And for goodness sake, don't think about succeeding EVERY time you focus on your goals—just imagine what would happen if you did!

It's All about You

Another mistake people often make when they first begin working on their BIG goals is to describe their goals in terms of how they want other people to change. "I want my husband to take me out more" or "I want my boss to treat me with more respect"

> "We all have the ability. The difference is how we use it."
> STEVIE WONDER

aren't goals—they're fantasies, and enjoyable as they might be, they won't change your life until they're backed up by action.

No matter how powerful our minds are, no one has yet found a way to control everything that happens to us or everything that other people do. But we do have a great deal of control over our own feelings and behavior. Goals like "I am going to go out at least three times a week" or "I will command more respect at work" put you back in the driver's seat.

Break Your Goals Down until It's Easy to Take Action

A movie actor friend of mine took the lead role in a West End play. Compared to movies, which are filmed in short scenes rarely lasting more than a couple of minutes, the idea of having to learn three hours' worth of continuous dialogue was overwhelming to him.

> "Nothing is particularly hard if you divide it into small jobs."
>
> HENRY FORD

When he asked me for help, the first thing I did was to get him to divide the play in half. I then had him divide each half into individual scenes. Suddenly he had a number of small pieces to work with rather than one big overwhelming one.

As he mastered each of the small pieces, it became easier and easier to put them together. Even when he was performing the play to rave reviews, he never thought about more than one small piece at a time.

When people first set their own BIG goals, they sometimes get a little bit freaked out by them and think they will never be able to achieve them. But by breaking them down into small enough chunks, you will find that you can achieve anything you set your mind to.

How small should each chunk be?

Small enough that you can take your very next action on it in the next 24 hours!

Four Simple Steps to Success

Here's all you need to remember:

1. Create goals BIG enough to get you out of bed in the morning.

2. Focus on what you want, and only what you want.

3. **Make sure your goals are all about you.**

4. **Break down your goals to make it easy to take action.**

Once you have designed a couple of BIG goals that are truly inspiring to you, you will find your life changing at an extraordinary rate. But in order to sustain this momentum, there is one more thing you need to do . . .

13.

Get the Action Habit!

The Master Key to Success

A friend of mine had just launched a new business idea in record time. When I asked him how he did it, he told me it was really quite simple.

> "You don't have to see the whole staircase—just take the first step."
> MARTIN LUTHER KING, JR.

"I realized that if I just spoke to five people a day about the project," he said, "that would be 150 people in a month. And I knew it was a good enough idea that if I talked to 150 people about it, somebody was bound to be interested."

What he said was particularly fascinating about the process was that for the first couple of days, he really had to push himself to phone people. Every time he picked up the phone, he felt an uncomfortable feeling in his stomach and heard his internal voice tell him there was no point in even trying, and that the other person could not possibly be interested. He got so sick of it that he said to himself "screw it," pushed himself past the feeling and straight into action. By the third day, the feeling of discomfort had lessened considerably, and it was becoming easier and easier to make the calls.

By the end of the first week, he felt the feelings of discomfort for less than a second before each call, and it became almost easier to pick up the phone and take action than not to. Before he even got to the fiftieth person he made the deal.

What was the key to his success?

He took action every single day until he reached his goal!

When you take action every day toward what you want, it gets easier and easier to take the next action the next day. This is because, like anything else you do repeatedly, taking action becomes a habit.

No one ever shows up to work naked, smacks themselves in the forehead and says, "I can't believe it—I forgot to get dressed this morning!"

This is because you have practiced getting dressed before leaving the house so many times that it has become a habit—a neurophysiological program in your nervous system.

When you apply the same simple logic to reaching your BIG goals, you will find yourself mastering the action habit. Simply write down your BIG goals somewhere you can see them. Take at least one action every day that takes you closer to achieving them. By doing at least one thing for each goal every day, you build an unstoppable momentum making it easier and easier to move in the direction you want.

The Wisdom of Uncertainty

Perhaps the biggest mistake people make that limits their confidence and effectiveness in situation after situation is to wait until they feel absolutely certain about something before taking action. Yet what sets high-achievers in every walk of life apart is that they have developed the habit of taking action *before* they feel completely ready.

> *"I am always doing things I can't do—that's how I get to do them."*
> PABLO PICASSO

Have you ever had an idea for a product or service and some time later you opened a magazine or walked in to a store and there was your idea? The difference between you and the person who did the service or created the product is simple: they took action.

You may say that you didn't take action because you weren't ready, but the real secret of the action habit is this:

**Truly successful people take action
before they feel ready!**

The action habit is a mind program that responds to the unknown by moving forward instead of holding back. While it does not ignore potential danger, it also doesn't give in to fear. Instead of waiting for certainty, the action habit encourages you to gather information and then to move forward a little bit before you're ready. Then, once you are already in action, you can course-correct as necessary to ensure you reach your goal.

Not only will the action habit get you where you want to go, it will ensure that you arrive there feeling more satisfied than ever before. Brain researcher Gregory Berns has demonstrated in a number of recent experiments that, contrary to most people's expectations, it is the feeling of uncertainty that holds the key to satisfaction in life.

People like what's familiar, but are rewarded for what's different. The more things happen the way we expect them to, the less our brains notice. But when we experience something new or unexpected, our brains light up and massive amounts of dopamine (your brain's "motivation chemical") are released. Then, when you achieve your goal, your brain rewards you by releasing serotonin (your brain's "happy chemical"). This in turn increases your motivation to do more new things in the future, and physically enhances the molecular struc-ture of your brain, increasing your capacity for even greater feelings of satisfaction.

Learned Helplessness

Many years ago, the Denver Zoo had a bear who lived in a cage that was no more than thirty feet long.

> "Argue for your limitations, and sure enough, they're yours."
> RICHARD BACH

All day he paced up and down inside the tiny cage. Eventually the zoo raised enough money to build a grand enclosure for the bear, with trees, rocks, and even a waterfall. The day finally came when the enclosure was finished and a crane lifted the bear in its cage into the enclosure. The bolts that held the cage together were removed and the bear stepped out into his brave new world.

What do you think happened? Did our bear friend live out the rest of his days in happiness and delight with his newfound freedom?

Sadly, no. Even though he was now in the lavish new surroundings, he continued to pace up and down in the same number of steps that he had while in his tiny cage until the day he died.

Like the bear, human beings all too quickly learn how to adapt to their limitations. This phenomenon, known by researchers as "learned helplessness," is one of the root causes of depression, inaction, and self-defeating behavior.

But the way out couldn't be simpler—take action on your goals, especially if you don't quite feel ready yet. Each time you successfully step outside your comfort zone by taking action before you are ready, your brain will reward you with increased doses of dopamine and increased feelings of confidence, satisfaction, and well-being.

And life will reward you as well . . .

14.

The Currency of the Gods

Taking a Quantum Leap Forward

Taking risks is an essential part of your journey toward success. But I have learned from my work with high-achievers and top athletes that there is a tremendous difference between confident risk-taking and foolish acts of self-endangerment.

> *"There are costs and risks to a program of action, but they are far less than the long-range risks and costs of comfortable inaction."*
>
> JOHN F. KENNEDY

Too many people stop themselves from doing something because it seems "too risky." But professional risk-takers aren't necessarily braver, just more prepared. They always go through some variation on the following three steps before going ahead: identifying the risk, assessing it, and going for it.

Here's how it all works . . .

1. Identify the potentially useful or unavoidable risk

There are essentially two types of risk—those that are imposed on us from the outside and those we choose to take on for ourselves in hopes of greater or accelerated reward.

You will know that an activity or course of action is risky in one of two ways—either because you intellectually know that it is risky, or because of the feeling of relative unease or discomfort that accompanies thinking about it.

2. Assess the balance between risk and reward

When bookmakers lay odds on sporting events or individual achievements, they make their decisions based on probabilities—how likely they think it is that the person they are laying odds on will succeed or fail. A simple tool you can use to do the same thing for yourself is based on generating two numbers, both on a scale from 1 to 10.

The first number represents the potential upside, or reward—i.e., how much of a positive impact, on a scale from 1 to 10, could taking the action or course of action have on your situation?

The second number represents the potential downside, or risk—i.e., how much of a negative impact, on a scale from 1 to 10, could taking the action or course of action have on your situation?

Here's the magic formula:

$$\textit{Potential Reward} - \textit{Potential Risk}$$
$$= \textit{Action Number}$$

A positive Action Number would suggest that a course of action might be worth taking; a negative

Action Number would suggest that a course of action might not be worth taking.

For example, some people attempt to cheat on their taxes. The upside for most of them is about a 1 (a few bucks saved); the potential downside (audits, fines, and possible jail time) is a 10.

On the other hand, if the benefit of asking someone out that you're highly attracted to is 10 (you could wind up getting married and having a family together) and the potential risk factor is 2 (they might say no), go for it!

3. Decide whether or not you are going to "take the risk"

Once you decide to take the risk, then take action!

Remember, great achievers have learned to take action even before they feel completely ready. This is the time when all the tools you have learned thus far in this book will really help you. Motivation is confidence in action—and confidence in action is what will carry you all the way to the life of your BIG goals and dreams!

Risk Taking for Fun and Profit

Read through the exercise before you do it for the first time . . .

1. Think of something you'd like to do, but it's a bit risky or a bit out of character for you to do it.

2. Take a couple of minutes to do some basic safety checks—make sure that you won't be harming yourself or anyone else in doing it.

3. Plan when to do it—ideally it will be today, but if not, try and find an opportunity within the next 72 hours.

4. When your moment comes, notice the familiar rush of adrenaline, tell yourself "aw, what the hell," and go for it!

5. Expect to be momentarily disoriented, but know that you will find all the resources you need as you proceed.

15.

Don't Take "No" for an Answer

Joanne, Kelly, and James

Joanne was a single mother living on public aid, struggling to make ends meet on 110 dollars a week.

> "Failure is an attitude, not an outcome."
>
> HARVEY MACKAY

She had just split with her partner, and decided to fill her time by working on an idea she'd had for a book for children. Every morning she sat in her local café and wrote; every afternoon she went home to look after her daughter, Jessica.

When she finally finished her manuscript, she sent it out into the world—where it was rejected by every major publisher in the United Kingdom, often with disparaging comments like "too long for children."

Finally, one publisher agreed to pay her a tiny advance and put the book out. Today, *Harry Potter* is one of the greatest literary success stories of all time, and Joanne "J.K." Rowling is one of the most widely read authors on the planet, worth three quarters of a billion dollars!

James, on the other hand, was an inventor. He had an idea for a new kind of product that he felt would change many housewives' lives for the better—only he couldn't get it to work. Five years and 5,127 attempts after he began, he had a working prototype—but still couldn't get anyone interested. Despite facing one rejection after another, he kept his dream alive. Finally, after ten years of determination and tenacious daily action, James Dyson launched what soon became the best-selling vacuum cleaner into the world.

Kelly was born to a mother who was only eighteen, but her athletic prowess brought her national attention at an early age. Despite her potential, she gave up competition to serve her country in the British army. Inspired by the sight of one of her former classmates competing at a world-class level, she returned to Great Britain and began to prepare for the Olympics.

And then tragedy struck. On top of some minor injuries, she was diagnosed with cancer. It seemed that once again her dreams would have to be put on the back burner, this time forever. Yet Kelly Holmes sprinted to victory twice at the Athens Olympics in 2004, only the third woman in history to win the double. Despite having to overcome an impoverished background, continual injuries, and even life-threatening illness, Dame Kelly Holmes is an inspiration to millions.

Resilience

What is it that allows a J.K. Rowling, James Dyson, or Kelly Holmes to keep going in the face of seemingly insurmountable odds?

Their refusal to take "no" for an answer from life or anyone else.

In some primitive tribes, the shaman could only become the keeper of wisdom and magic and healing after he or she had been wounded in battle. It was believed that it was through the shaman's wounds that

> "If you're going through hell—keep going."
> WINSTON CHURCHILL

powerful wisdom would enter. This is in line with nature's wisdom, which forms our scars out of the strongest tissue in the body, even though they might be the result of deep injury.

Yet most of us think of failure as a reason to give up, treating each adversity as another excuse for not getting where we really want to go. The truth is, failure is simply a matter of perception.

Over the years a number of people have said to me, "I tried hypnosis to quit smoking and it didn't work." When I ask them if it was really true that they hadn't stopped smoking even for a single day, they always reply with something like, "Well, I stopped for a few months, but then I started again. It's a shame it didn't work."

"What do you mean it didn't work?" I tell them. "Of course it worked!"

If you can stop for a month, you can stop for two, or six or a year or forever. But not if you stop yourself first.

Can you imagine if parents treated their children like that when they were learning to walk? Every time the child fell over, they would tell him to give up. "Oh, well, Timmy—I guess you'll never be a walker."

So let's look at that. Think about something you think you failed at in your own life. Did you really "fail"?

Remember, not winning is not the same as failure. Neither is things not turning out exactly the way that you wanted, or getting turned down by someone you wanted something from.

The first question you need to ask yourself is this:

So what?

So you didn't win. So it didn't turn out exactly like you wanted. So you got turned down. So what?

You're still alive—and tomorrow you've got another chance to make something even more wonderful happen. Not only that, you have learned lessons that will help you to succeed in the future.

High-achievers see what other people call "failure" as no more than a temporary setback and get excited about finding new ways to overcome the challenge and get back on track for success.

After accepting that things didn't work out the way they'd hoped, they ask themselves questions like:

What's unique about this problem?

How can I use this to my advantage?

What do I need to do to succeed?

In my training seminars, we take the participants through an exercise in taking back control over their perceptions of the events of their lives.

For example:

"I pay too much tax."

"You must make a lot of money."

"My husband is always criticizing me."

"He must really care about you."

At the extreme end of the scale, a participant once said in a sorrowful voice, "My wife left me for another man." Everyone went quiet for a few moments, until one of the women in the group said quietly, "Well, I guess now *he's* stuck with her!" Laughter broke out around the group, and the man was able to shift into a more resourceful state.

It is important to remember that this is not meant as a therapeutic intervention or a suggestion that we should not treat the significant events in our lives with the seriousness they merit; it is a training exercise in creating greater flexibility in our thinking.

Do this now . . .

On the Sunny Side of the Street

1. Think of something "bad" that happened to you.
2. Now, come up with at least five ways in which it could be perceived as a positive—the more ridiculous, the better!

Bouncing Back from Adversity

When I ask people what stops them from achieving their goals, they will often recall times from the past when they failed at something similar and then watch internal movies of themselves reliving those failures again and again. Thinking about past failures over and over is a sure way to recreate them, because we always get more of what we focus on. That's why it's important to recode any past negative experiences that still cause us stress in the present.

> "Let me tell you the secret that has led me to my goal: my strength lies solely in my tenacity."
>
> LOUIS PASTEUR

It's fine to remember that something bad happened and learn from it, but any experiences that still carry a heavy emotional charge can act as obstacles to your success and slow you down.

One American research study showed that people who bounce back quickly following challenges and setbacks have an unconscious habit of perceiving delays, mistakes, and even the motives of other people in the best possible light.

Here is a wonderful technique you can use to take away the negative change of any bad experience and leave yourself feeling stronger than before . . .

Building Resilience

Read through the exercise before you do it for the first time . . .

1. Imagine you are sitting in a movie theater, with a tiny screen some distance from you.

2. Make a black-and-white still picture on the screen of a past mistake or failure that you think means something about your ability to succeed in the future.

3. Watch the movie of that event backward as if it were happening to someone else. Keep running it backward faster and faster until thinking of the event doesn't stress you anymore.

4. Now make the screen much bigger and a movie of yourself succeeding in the future. Make it big, bold, and beautiful, in full color with a thumping soundtrack.

5. Step into the movie and feel the feelings of confidence, motivation, and success as you imagine everything going perfectly the way you want!

16.

Overcoming Overwhelm

Life Happens

Even though you will achieve more and more success as you practice these techniques and listen to
the CD, there will inevitably
be times when "life happens."
Perhaps a business deal will
fall through, or you will get
into an argument with your
partner, or you'll have so many
balls up in the air that they all seem to fall to the
ground at once.

> "Being defeated is often
> a temporary condition.
> Giving up is what
> makes it permanent."
>
> MARILYN VOS SAVANT

When this does happen (and it happens to everyone at some point), the most important thing you
can do is forgive yourself. It's not punishment for
something you did wrong or for making bad pictures
in your head. It's just an inevitable part of life. The
tool I am going to share with you in this chapter is
the most reliable one I know for overcoming overwhelm and returning yourself quickly and easily to a
state of quiet confidence regardless of what is going
on around you.

Thought Field Therapy (TFT) was developed by the
innovative American scientist Dr. Roger Callahan.
Independent scientific research on Callahan's tech-

niques show that they work most of the time for most people in helping to reduce emotional overwhelm.

What we are about to do involves tapping on certain acupuncture points on your body. The code for any stressful feeling is stored like a computer program in your brain. By thinking about what is worrying you while tapping on each point in exactly the sequence I am going to describe, you will be able to quickly reduce your levels of anxiety, stress, or overwhelm and get on with your life.

This process may seem a bit strange at first, but it works. In a moment I want you to think of a stressful experience. By the time you finish following my instructions, your stress will disappear. It will seem like magic, but in fact it's hard science.

You will need to be able to really concentrate for a few minutes, as it is important that you continue thinking about the emotion you have chosen as you go through this process and reduce the feeling . . .

(Before you do this technique read through each step so that you know what to do.)

1. Focus on whatever it is that you are feeling overwhelmed about. Now, rate the stress on a scale of 1–10, with 1 being the lowest and 10 the highest. This is important, because in a moment we will see how far you've reduced it. You must continue to think about whatever it is that was bothering you throughout the sequence that follows.

2. Take two fingers of either hand and tap about ten times just above one of your eyebrows.

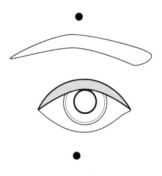

3. Now, tap under the same eye.

4. Tap under your collarbone.

5. Keep thinking about what was bothering you and tap under your armpit.

6. Next, tap on the "karate chop" point on the side of your hand.

7. Place that hand in front of you and tap on the back of it at the point between the knuckles of your ring finger and your little finger. (Continue tapping that point and thinking about the stressful situation throughout steps 8–13.)

8. Close your eyes, then open them.

9. Look down to the right, back to center, and then down to the left.

10. Rotate your eyes round 360 degrees clockwise, then 360 degrees counterclockwise.

11. Still thinking about what was stressful to you and tapping, hum the first few lines of "Happy Birthday" out loud.

12. Now count out loud from 1 to 5. (1, 2, 3, 4, 5)

13. Now once again hum the first few lines of "Happy Birthday" out loud.

14. Repeat steps 2–6. Still thinking about what was overwhelming to you, tap above the eyebrow, under the eye, under your collarbone, under your armpit, and on the karate chop point.

Okay, let's stop and check—on a scale from 1 to 10, what number is the feeling at now?

If the feeling of overwhelm hasn't completely gone yet, simply go back through the entire sequence again until it does. It may take as many as two or even three times before you have completely eliminated the feeling, although most people report getting the feeling down to a manageable level on their first or second try.

Remember, if you have run through this process several times and the feeling hasn't gone away completely, tune in to the message it is bringing you from your unconscious mind. In addition, you can repeat this process as often as you like.

17.

Create a Compelling Positive Future

It's About Time

Simply by having taken the time to design your BIG goals and take action, your life will begin to improve. But we are now going to use the power of your unconscious mind to take the whole game to another level and begin creating "automatic" success.

> "My interest is in the future because I am going to spend the rest of my life there."
>
> CHARLES KETTERING

In order to do this, you need to first notice your brain's own unique way of representing time. Without thinking about it, point to the future. Now, point to the past.

Notice the direction that time moves for you. Does the future extend out in front of you with past behind you? Or is the past on the left and the future on the right?

There are no right or wrong answers—however your brain codes time is perfect for you. Do the following exercise to become even more clear about your own internal "timeline" . . .

Discovering Your Timeline

Read through the exercise before you do it for the first time . . .

1. Think of something that you do each day, like brushing your teeth or having your breakfast. When you picture yourself doing that tomorrow, is the image in front of you, to the right, or to the left? How far away is it? Point to it now . . .

2. Next, think about doing the same activity next week. Is the picture farther to the right or to the left? In front of you or behind you? Closer or farther away? Once again, point to where you "see" the image in your mind.

   What about last week? Where do you picture doing that same activity one week ago?

3. Now think about doing the same activity one month into the future. Is the picture closer or farther away? More to the right or the left? In front or behind? Higher or lower?

   What about one month ago, in the past? Where do you picture having done that same activity then?

4. Finally, imagine yourself doing that same activity six months into the future. Where is that picture—closer or farther? Left or right? Higher or lower?

   How about six months ago—point to that image now . . .

5. Imagine that all these images are connected by a line—like doing a giant connect-the-dots puzzle in your mind. This is your "timeline"—the way your unconscious mind represents time.

Programming Your Mind for "Automatic Success"

When you have a sufficiently compelling future, all of your resources are automatically directed toward bringing that future about. And the really wonderful thing is that you will find yourself moving toward that future every single day.

This next exercise will assist you in programming a compelling future into your unconscious mind. Used in conjunction with the CD, it will supercharge all your efforts for success . . .

> "If you really want something, you can figure out how to make it happen."
>
> CHER

When I did this with a client recently, he made an image of himself sitting at dinner with his family and friends. They were all sitting around celebrating his latest success at work. There was an incredible sense of prosperity about them, like they never needed to worry about money again. They were planning their luxury vacation in the south of France and joking about how much fun they were going to have sipping champagne and soaking up the sun. What he really enjoyed about the picture was that he seemed so grounded and happy in himself—

there was a real sense of having "arrived" both spiritually and materially.

Creating Your Future Now

Read through the exercise before you do it for the first time . . .

1. Imagine it's a year in the future and you have had the best year of your life.

    What has happened in your relationships, career, health, finances, spiritual life? Which of your BIG goals have you achieved? Which ones have you made significant progress toward? What new thinking and behaviors have you practiced? Who are you becoming?

2. Now, create an ideal scene that represents all that you most want to happen in your positive future. Make sure you can see yourself in that future looking really positive and happy. It can be realistic or symbolic.

    Design your "ideal scene" now. Where are you? Who are you with? Which successes are you most aware of? What do you like about it most?

3. Take that image and put it onto your timeline one year into the future. Make sure the image is really big, bright, bold, and colorful. You'll know you're doing it right because it feels really good just to imagine it. ➤

4. Next, you are going to fill in the blanks between then and now.

   Make a slightly smaller picture and place it a few months before the big picture of what will need to happen before that.

   Make an even smaller picture and place it a few months before that picture of what will need to happen before that.

   Make an even smaller picture and place it a few months before that picture of what will need to happen before.

   You should now have a succession of pictures connecting the present with your positive, compelling future. The images should get progressively bigger with better and better things happening in them.

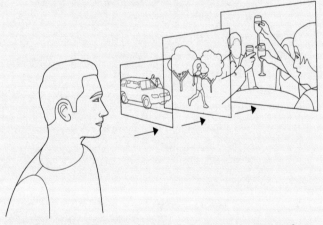

5. Look at those pictures and let your unconscious mind lock in the roadmap to your automatic success over the next year.

6. Now, float up and out of your body and into each picture. Take a few moments to fully experience each step you will be taking on the path to greater success.

7. When you get to the big picture of your ideal scene, really allow yourself to enjoy experiencing it fully. What will it be like to have everything you want?

8. Finally, come back to the present and look out once again at your future timeline. You can feel confident in the knowledge that you have now created a map for your unconscious to use as a guide in bringing about the future you are longing to create!

18.

Your Daily Action Plan for Success

Everybody's Doing It

Years ago I was talking to Olympic Decathlon gold-medalist Daley Thompson about sports psychology. I asked him if he ever used any himself. He replied that he didn't really see the point because he didn't believe in it. So I asked him if he ever thought about a race before he ran it. He looked at me and with strong conviction said, "I think about every single step again and again. I know exactly what I am going to do and I go out and do it!"

> "If all you did was tell a lamppost your goals for each day, they would still be far more likely to happen."
>
> MICHAEL NEILL

The same thing is true of any champion or top performer I have ever worked with—whether they practice these techniques consciously or unconsciously, they practice them perfectly until they become what they have practiced.

If you want to take your life to the next level, that is all you need to do. In fact, just by embarking on a program of self-development, your life will begin to improve.

In the 1930s, a famous study was done about contributory factors to efficiency in the workplace. A team of social scientists led by Harvard Business School professor Elton Mayo went to factories to assess, among other things, the effect of increased lighting on efficiency in assembly lines. As was the typical procedure of the day, three groups were observed.

The first group was given increased lighting as they went about their repetitive assembly tasks; the second was given decreased lighting; the third, or "control," group was simply observed going about their work in the usual manner. What happened next confounded the observers . . .

As expected, the group with increased lighting experienced a measurable increase in efficiency and well-being on the job. However, the increase in efficiency and well-being was almost identically matched in both of the other groups being observed.

After further experimentation, the conclusion reached by Professor Mayo and his colleagues was that the single most important factor in positively affecting the efficiency and well-being of employees was *the feeling that attention was being paid to their efforts.*

What Gets Measured Gets Done

According to the American Society of Training and Development, the likelihood of you doing something if you agree to check in with someone for accountability rises from only 40 percent (without the check-in) to a whopping 95 percent!

Similarly, by taking the extra one minute a day to track your actions toward your BIG goals, you will massively increase the likelihood of your success.

> "Success is the sum of small efforts repeated day in and day out."
> ROBERT COLLIER

Here's a sample chart you can use to track your progress. If you are wondering why I've only put enough space for five goals, it's because if you have time to take daily action on more than five goals, they're almost certainly not BIG enough!

Make a copy of the chart and write in your BIG goals. Each day, simply put a check in the appropriate box when you have taken at least one action toward that goal for the day.

While this may seem too simple to be truly effective, I cannot emphasize enough the power of momentum I have seen people create in their lives as a result of doing this exercise. Dramatic positive changes often begin occurring in only a few short weeks!

Your Daily Action Plan for Success

BIG Goal	Mon	Tues	Wed	Thurs	Fri	Sat	Sun
1.							
2.							
3.							
4.							
5.							

Confidence
in the
Real World

19.

Public Speaking

Making Powerful Presentations

The fear of public speaking is now the largest phobia in the western world. It usually get installed at school

> *"Ask yourself: if I had only sixty seconds on the stage, what would I absolutely have to say to get my message across?"*
>
> JEFF DEWAR

where we are told to read in front of the class and a teacher points out all our mistakes rather than reinforces how well we are doing. Other kids laughing and pointing assists in the installation, ensuring we are in a strong enough negative state that the association between fear, shame, embarrassment, and speaking in public has stayed with us until now, even if it hasn't always stopped us from getting up and doing it.

Yet there are only three things you need to do in order to feel easy and comfortable making powerful presentations in front of even the largest group:

1. **Manage your state.**

2. **Know your content.**

3. **Speak with passion.**

1. Manage your state

Many years ago, one of Britain's leading actresses came to see me. When she told me she was suffering from stage fright, I was shocked.

I said "Hang on, you're one of the best—how could you have stage fright?"

She replied, "When you get to my position, the pressure to succeed is even greater."

It really struck me at that moment just how little confidence has to do with experience, and just how much it has to do with the way we use our minds. Someone else could have used their vast experience and history of past success to build an unshakeable feeling of ease and comfort; she had used hers to compound her fears.

In order to help her, I asked her to imagine that she was going to take a day off from the stage fright. I would be taking over her fear for the day. I then asked her what I would have to do to make myself feel frightened on stage the way she did.

Here was her strategy:

1. First, she would walk on to the stage and then imagine the critics thinking all sorts of harsh things about her performance, like "She didn't deliver that line very well, did she?"

2. Next, her body would tense up in response to the negative internal dialogue and she would make some small mistake.

3. Finally, she would imagine the critics saying something even worse, like, "Oooh—she's past her best." The more she imagined the critic's response, the more real mistakes she began to make.

Although she had no idea what the critics were really saying about her, or even if they were really in the audience, by imagining them saying terrible things she was creating a self-fulfilling prophecy.

As her self-talk was having such a powerful effect upon her performance, I decided it would be a good idea to use it to help her. After all, if she could imagine people saying horrible things about her, she must be able to imagine them saying positive things.

I asked her to imagine walking out on stage and hearing the critics saying all kinds of positive things in their minds, like, "What a fine experienced actress—what a marvelous performance!" If she did make a mistake, she would imagine them saying, "How well recovered—bravo!"

We simply rehearsed this in her mind over and over again until it became the new program. The

next time she walked out on the stage the new positive self-talk began to happen automatically.

And when the critics really did come to see the
show, they gave her rave reviews!

Here is an exercise you can use to enhance your
state anytime you speak . . .

The Voice of Confidence

Read through the exercise before you do it for the first
time . . .

1. Imagine how your voice would sound if you
   were totally confident right now. Alternatively,
   imagine the voice of a confident, passionate
   person you enjoy listening to.

2. Now start to match your voice out loud with the
   confident voice inside your head.

3. Do it a sentence at a time. Imagine the
   confident voice inside your head saying
   something like, "This is how I sound when I am
   confident." Then say it out loud at the same
   time, doing your best to match the energy
   and tone.

It might feel a little strange at first, but you will
soon start to feel completely comfortable speaking
aloud in your more confident tone of voice.

2. Know your content

While it is certainly possible to bluff your way through a presentation, I don't recommend it. There's something about having done your homework and knowing what you're talking about that comes across as a vibration of competence to your audience.

But knowing your content is very different from reciting a script. In fact, the real benefit of knowing your content is this:

> *When you know what you're talking about, you don't need to know what you're going to say.*

One of my own most profound learning experiences about this came many years ago. When I first started teaching NLP with Dr. Richard Bandler, the man who created the field, I would prepare my mental script thoroughly by planning out *everything* I was going to say and do in advance.

One day just as I was about to go on stage, Richard suggested that I teach a different module from the one I usually did. I must have looked worried, because he laughed and asked me how long I'd been doing hypnosis and NLP.

I told him I'd been doing it for nearly ten years, and he laughed again.

"You have all the knowledge on this subject that you need," Richard said. "You just have to be in the right state and the words and ideas will flow. After all, if you were sitting talking with good friends about it, you wouldn't be worried, would you?"

He then asked me to remember a time where I'd done just that. When I started to feel that relaxed feeling in my body, he had me take that feeling with me as I imagined talking to the group, feeling relaxed and at ease.

Although I still didn't feel completely ready, my intro music started to play and for the first time I walked on to the stage with nothing formally pre-pared. Not only was it one of the best classes I'd ever taught, it was the most relaxed I had ever felt in front of a group. Everything flowed beautifully from that moment on!

3. Speak with passion

Even though we can speak about anything if we have to, whenever I am speaking publicly I make it a point to find an emotional connection with what it is I am going to be talking about.

The value of this practice became clear to me when I attended an awards ceremony called "The Pride of Britain." People who had committed acts of extraordinary bravery or made unique contributions to society were being publicly acknowledged. What was truly fascinating was that although many of the people receiving the awards had never spoken in front of an audience before, they were each able to totally captivate the audience, simply because they were truly passionate about what they had done.

To help me find my passion before I speak, I ask myself two simple questions:

What is the essence of my message to the audience?

What experience do I want them to have from listening to my talk?

Of course, passion is also a state—and like any state, you can create it any time you choose . . .

Your Ideal Performance State

Read through the exercise before you do it for the first time . . .

1. Think of a presentation you are going to be making in the next few weeks. If you don't have one scheduled, think about any upcoming performance situation where you want to be at your best.

2. If it was entirely up to you, how would you like to feel during your presentation or performance?
   Example:
   Confident, passionate, and fun

3. Imagine a circle on the floor of any color. Fill it up with the feelings you desire. You can do this by thinking of a time you felt that way in the past or by using your body "as if" you already feel that way now.
   Example:
   I fill my circle with confidence by standing in a confident posture and speaking to myself in a confident tone of voice. I add in a sense of passion by thinking about a cause I am deeply passionate about until I can feel those feelings in my body. I remember a time when I was laughing and joking with friends, and put that in the circle for a sense of fun.

4. Step into the circle and let the feelings spread through your body. As you feel them, visualize yourself doing the thing you want to do. ➤

When the feelings start to fade, step out of the circle and "recharge" it with emotion, then step back in.

5. Repeat steps 3 and 4 until you automatically feel the way you want to feel while imagining and/or doing the thing you want to do!

As with any of the exercises in this book, you become what you practice—and the more you practice being relaxed and confident as you do the things you want to do, the more relaxed and confident you become!

20.

Business Success

The Smell of Desperation

Have you ever been around someone who wanted something from you so badly that it was creepy? Whether it was a salesman in pursuit of your money or someone in pursuit of sex, there is something about neediness that is off-putting to even the most generous-hearted people.

In the performing arts, this is often called "the sickly smell of desperation," and is contrasted with "the sweet smell of success." Whether this is a metaphor or an actual biochemical event inside the body, the fact is that when you approach people from a place of need, it is much harder for them to respond positively to your request.

The key to dropping desperation is understanding this:

Desperation is a state—and like any state, it can be created or collapsed by the pictures, sounds, and self-talk in your head.

Do this now . . .

The Desperation Destroyer

Read through the exercise before you do it for the first time . . .

1. Think about something you feel needy or desperate about. It could be money, a sale, or even a relationship you would like to have.

2. Notice the pictures, sounds, and self-talk you have associated with this situation. If you are having trouble, make it up!

3. Take charge of your internal world! Take the pictures, push them off into the distance and fade them out. Turn down the volume on the sounds and self-talk until you are feeling relatively calm about whatever it is you were desperate about.

4. Now, create a "success collage" of all the good things you have in your life. Imagine dozens of pictures of the people you like and who like you, times when you have been successful in the past, and anything else you are grateful for having in your life. Replay any positive compliments you have received. Fill your mind with positive words, sounds, and images.

5. Finally, imagine a tiny space opening up somewhere in the bottom half of your success collage. Fill the space with a tiny representation of whatever it is you used to feel needy or desperate about.

6. In the future, you will only think about this thing in the context of all the wonderful things you already have going for you in your life!

As with any of the exercises you have done thus far in the book, this one becomes easier and easier with practice. The more you are aware of the "big picture" of your life, the less overwhelming or important any one aspect will become.

Leadership

When Steve Jobs and Steve Wozniak were trying to build the prototype for the Apple computer, they attempted to get Atari and Hewlett-Packard interested. They even offered to give the companies all the rights in exchange for funding and a nominal salary. Not only were they rejected, Hewlett-Packard actually said, "We don't need you—you haven't finished college yet!"

Similarly, Fed Ex, CNN, and Post-it notes all failed focus groups simply because they were counterintuitive. The majority of people in the world are not leaders or innovators, so to ask them about ideas that are outside of their normal frames of reference is pointless.

> "My grandfather once told me that there were two kinds of people: those who do the work and those who take the credit. He told me to try to be in the first group; there was much less competition."
>
> INDIRA GANDHI

As a leader you must expect resistance and even rejection, because they are the price of innovation. So if you are going to be a leader, you're going to have to be willing to lead.

In psychologist Robert Cialdini's classic book *Influence: Science and Practice*, he describes an experiment done on the streets of Chicago.

A pristine new car was left in a "bad" neighborhood overnight. When the researchers returned the next morning, the car was still there, pristine and intact. A few weeks later, a similar car was left in the same neighborhood—this time with one window broken. By morning, all four tires had been stolen and the car had been completely demolished.

What happened? Why was one car left alone and the other destroyed?

The answer comes in a principle of influence Cialdini calls "social proof"—the idea that when people do not know what to do or how to behave, they look to someone in their peer group to "teach" them what to do. As soon as one person has established the acceptable pattern of behavior, everyone else follows.

Understanding the power of social proof gives us a valuable insight into our ability to assume a leadership role in nearly any work situation. A large part of the impact we have on our environments and our teams is down to our ability to do one thing—to "go first" with the kind of behavior we want to encourage in others.

Want your team at work to be willing to experiment more, even if they make mistakes?

Go first by openly experimenting, making mistakes, and making it okay.

Want your clients to tell you the truth about what's going on with them?

Go first by telling them the truth about what's going on with you, even when the truth makes you look like less than a perfect manager, salesperson, or coach.

There are many examples of mistakes made by leaders who forgot to open their minds to possibility:

In the early nineteenth century, the scientific authorities of the day tried to stop steam engines from being developed because they believed that a human being that exceeded the incredible speed of 30 miles an hour would suffocate and be crushed by the force gravity.

In 1899, Charles H. Duell, Commissioner of Patents, recommended closing the patent office because "everything that can be invented has been invented."

In 1946, Daryl Zanuck, Jr., the head of 20th Century Fox, said, "Television won't be able to hold on to any market it captures in the first six months. People will soon get tired of staring at a plywood box every night."

Jim Denny of the Nashville music venue the Grand Ole Opry fired Elvis Presley after his first performance, saying, "You ain't goin' nowhere, son. You ought to go back to drivin' a truck."

Decca Records rejected The Beatles, saying, "We don't like their sound. Groups of guitars are on their way out."

Thomas Watson, Jr., then president of IBM, predicted there would be a world market for "about five" computers.

And even Bill Gates was not immune, arguing in 1981 that "640K ought to be enough for anyone."

The Simplest Skill for Success

All of the tools you have learned so far come back to four basic skills:

1. **Make confident pictures of yourself succeeding.**

2. **Speak to yourself in a confident, positive tone of voice.**

3. **Move your body with confidence.**

4. **Take action before you're ready.**

But in business, there's a fifth skill that is equally if not more important:

Be who you are!

So many businesses and businesspeople spend all their time trying to be all things to all people that they are continually off balance, spinning plate after plate and hoping the whole lot doesn't come crashing down around their ears.

Yet if they understood this basic business principle, their lives would be significantly easier and their customers would be considerably happier.

When you're being who you are, as a businessperson or a business, some people will want what you've got and some won't. But as Jack Canfield, creator of the billion-dollar *Chicken Soup for the Soul* publishing empire, says, "Some will, some won't, so what . . . someone's waiting!"

Someone for Everyone

So here's a question for you. You can feel free to answer this in relation to any product or service that you are selling, but the question is this:

Do you think there is someone out there who wants what you have to offer?

If your answer is no, then you've got some work to do on "product development," especially if the product is you. But if your answer is "yes," then I've got another question for you . . .

Where are they?

Perhaps an even better question is:

How can you find them as quickly and easily as possible?

The answer is simple: find out who they are NOT as quickly as possible.

Here's an exercise from my success coach, Michael Neill . . .

Finding Your Ideal Clients and Customers

Read through the exercise before you do it for the first time . . .

1. Make a list of exactly twenty names of people or companies who might want what you have.

2. The objective of the game is to get rid of anyone on the list who does NOT want to work with or buy from you. Get in touch with each person on the list and get a "yes" or "no" as quickly as possible—don't take "maybe" for an answer!

   Remember, the objective of the game is to get the list down to zero as quickly as possible. Enjoy rejecting them for a change!

3. Give yourself a score at the end of the day, based on the number of names left on your list.

Scoring Table:

18-20   You're obviously not really going for it yet.
        Take a risk and get started!

13-17   This is about average for most people. Does
        slow and steady really win the race? If you
        think so, then celebrate! If not, crank up the
        confidence and get back into action!

8-12   You are well on your way to success. (If
        you've accidentally found someone who does
        want to buy from you, you can take them off
        the list as well.)

4-7   Clearly you've gone beyond pleasure into
        artistry. My compliments to the chef!

0-3   WARNING! WARNING! SUCCESS ALERT!
        SUCCESS ALERT! WARNING!

Keep track of your scores—if you can get down to 0 five working days in a row, you will have transformed your business and become far more confident than before.

21.

Dating
and Sex

Social Confidence

When it comes to confidence in the real world, the number one thing people want is to feel more comfortable socializing, particularly with people they are sexually attracted to. In this section, I will share some of the most important things I have learned about creating an abundance of social confidence, along with some specific techniques you can use to feel more naturally confident in social situations.

> *"Confidence contributes more to conversation than wit."*
>
> FRANÇOIS DE LA ROCHEFOUCAULD

Simon Cowell, one of the most confident people I know, told me that his father taught him that the key to success with other people was simply to imagine that everyone has a sign above their heads with the words "make me feel important" written on it in big bold letters.

So the most valuable thing of all to remember is this: The key to social confidence is to put the majority of your attention OUTSIDE of yourself and onto the person or people you are with.

In order to do that, you will need to feel comfortable enough with yourself that you don't have to continually monitor what is going on with you.

From Self-conscious to Self-confident

The comedian Buddy Hackett used to talk about the key to a great performance being the ability to "turn down the monitor." The monitor is that part of your mind that is continually monitoring how you're doing during a performance. When his monitor was turned up high, he was paying more attention to the pictures and self-talk inside his head than what was going on around him. During a really great show, the monitor was turned down so low that he could feel all his good feelings but keep the majority of his attention on the people around him. The lower the monitor, the better the performance.

In the same way, your ability to perform well in social, dating, and even sexual situations is largely a function of your ability to turn down the monitor and give your full attention to the person or people you are with.

There are only two things you need to do to bring your natural confidence to the fore in social, dating, and sexual situations:

1. **Upgrade your pictures and self-talk.**

2. **Pump up your state.**

1. Upgrade your pictures and self-talk

My friend kept talking about this woman he liked as if she was completely unattainable. He really wanted to go out with her, but every time he was around her he would become completely tongue-tied.

I noticed that whenever he spoke about her, he gestured in front of his face as if he was describing a picture.

When I asked him what the picture was, he didn't think he was looking at anything. But when I had him repeat the gestures and take another look at what he was imagining, he was making a big, bright, colorful picture of the woman standing tall like a goddess in his mind. In addition, he heard his internal voice saying, "Wow, she's the most beautiful woman in the world—why would she want to go out with some-body like me?"

No wonder he felt daunted about speaking with her!

I had him shrink the image right down until it fit into the palm of his hand, like shrinking an 8 × 10 down to a wallet-size photograph. Suddenly, his body posture completely changed. He looked surprised but far more confident.

"That's weird," he said to me. "I'm not scared of her anymore."

I then told him to look at the new picture in his mind and tell himself, "It's possible she would go out with me," in his most confident internal tone of voice. At first he thought it was a ridiculous thing to say, but he did as I had asked. I had him repeat it again and again until the smile on his face let me know that his state had completely changed.

The next time he saw her, he felt much more comfortable, although he told me he had to go inside his mind and change his pictures a few more times before it became automatic. Although he didn't yet feel completely at ease, he felt comfortable enough to tell himself "what the hell!" and ask her out on a date. (She said yes!)

2. Pump up your state

Once someone is feeling less daunted by the person or people they want to spend time with, it's time to create some new powerfully positive associations.

When I do this with a client, I begin by having them think about people around whom they already feel confident and comfortable. When they are beginning to feel those feelings in their body, we create an association between those feelings and the person they would like to feel comfortable with in the future.

If this is someone to whom they are sexually attracted, I then have them imagine someone who for them is a role model of social and sexual confidence—it can be someone they know, but more usually people choose a movie star, someone like Catherine Zeta Jones, Sean Connery, Cameron Diaz, or George Clooney.

Finally, we put it all together and mentally rehearse being in the same social situations but with these brand new "pumped-up" positive feelings.

Let's do this now . . .

Ready for Romance, Part One

Read through the exercise before you do it for the first time . . .

1. Who are you most comfortable being yourself with? Is it a certain group of friends, or members of your family?

   Whoever it is, go back to a particularly pleasant experience of spending time with them. Allow those feelings to come back now and use them to create a "Romantic Confidence Switch." Just put the thumb and middle finger of either hand together while you are feeling these feelings and build the association.

2. What are some other ways you'd like to feel? My clients often choose things like "relaxed," "not scared of being judged," and "permission to be myself."

3. Imagine someone who for you is a model of social and sexual confidence. Imagine them speaking confidently to the person or people you would like to be more comfortable with.

   When you're ready, step into that model so you're seeing through their eyes, hearing through their ears, and feeling what it feels like to be as socially and sexually confident and self-assured as they are.

   Once again, put together the thumb and middle finger of either hand, adding these feelings to your Romantic Confidence Switch, and keep doing it until you feel as confident as they do.

When you have created your Romantic Confidence Switch, it's time to put it to use. While you could just use it as an "in the moment" tool to instantly feel more relaxed and confident when you are with the person, it's even more powerful to use it to program your mind for success.

Every time you run through this movie in your mind, you are programming yourself for success. When you are actually with the person, you will be able to relax and allow your natural confidence to guide you as you make them the most important person in your world!

Ready for Romance, Part Two

Read through the exercise before you do it for the first time . . .

1. Hit your Romantic Confidence Switch by putting your thumb and middle finger together. Pump up the state by making the pictures and sounds bigger, bolder, and brighter. Make sure you're speaking to yourself in your most confident tone of voice and using your body in a posture of easy confidence and success.

2. While in this powerful positive state, imagine a movie of you getting along extremely well with the other person. Imagine the sign over their head that says, "Make me feel important." See them laughing, smiling, or whatever it is that lets you know they're having a wonderful time with you.

3. Now throw in a challenge or two as well, and watch yourself handling them easily and perfectly too. Keep imagining it all going perfectly the way you want it to.

   If you need to, put in your role model as a substitute to see how they would handle the challenge, then put yourself back in the picture.

4. When you've run through the movie a few times, step into it so you're seeing through your eyes, hearing through your ears, and enjoying the good feelings of being at your best when it matters most.

193

22.

Leaving a Bad Situation

When Is Enough Enough?

I am wondering if you are the person I've written this chapter for—the person in a situation so bad that if anyone had told you it would happen to you, you would have laughed or been insulted.

But somehow, you've wound up here. Maybe you're depressed or stuck in a dead-end job, wondering whether you'll ever get sick and tired of feeling sick and tired. Maybe you're in an emotionally or physically abusive relationship, wondering how in the hell something like this could happen to someone like you.

It happens the way any unconscious pattern happens—bit by bit and day by day. If you throw a frog in to a pot of hot water it will jump out. Put it in a pot of cold water and heat it up slowly and the frog will stay in there until he's dead.

> *"Twenty years from now you will be more disappointed by the things that you didn't do than by the ones you did do."*
>
> MARK TWAIN

But I've got some good news—the way out is fast, direct, and immediate. Even if you're not quite ready, your new life can begin just a few minutes from now . . .

Taking Yourself over the Threshold

Richard Bandler has a friend who runs a shelter for women who have been abused by their partners. His friend couldn't find a way to persuade the women to stop giving their partners just one more chance. Many of them went back again and again, and got abused again and again.

Eventually one of the women was killed by her partner. That's when Richard was asked to help. He started by going and interviewing women who had successfully left abusive relationships.

He wanted to find out what exactly had taken place in them that allowed them to leave. He made a fascinating discovery. They all ran a similar pattern in their minds. They would think about all the bad things that had happened to them again and again, one after another until the bad memories began to join up so there wasn't any space between them.

The more the memories joined up, the more intense and uncomfortable the feelings got, until whenever they thought about the situation they used to feel stuck in, all they could remember was the pain and fear. Any thought of the "not so bad" times was gone.

The cumulative effect of all these negative memories at once broke their attachment to the idealized view they had of their partner. It was the straw that broke the camel's back. They had crossed a threshold. They simply couldn't go back to thinking of their ex-partner as a "nice guy with a temper" any more. From that moment on, there was no longer any question of whether or not they would go back.

Richard decided to teach the other women in the shelter how to remember all the bad times all strung together, so that they could feel their full effect. Essentially he used a psychological mechanism that is already in us. However rather than wait for months or even years for it to activate, he showed them how to activate it immediately, before any further injuries.

The following technique is derived from Richard's work and many of the people I have used it with have said that it was the single most powerful action they took to free themselves from their attachment to an individual or situation that was causing them harm. They have said things like, "I don't have any feelings toward my ex now," "My ex feels like someone I used to know a long time ago," "Okay, it's turned off the overwhelming feelings, I can handle it now."

One client reported back to me that doing it just one single time had wiped out his overwhelming feelings. That gave his confidence a real boost, because he knew that even if any feelings of longing did return, he had a sure-fire way to get rid of them.

Here is the technique in its entirety. Part of its power comes from the speed at which you run it. So it is especially important to really take the time to read through it properly before you do it. If you have to stop to figure out the next step, you will lose momentum. So decide now whether you are ready for a radical change in your feelings and read it through carefully before you start.

The Threshold Technique

Read through the exercise before you do it for the first time . . .

1. Call to mind a picture of yourself with your ex when you were in love. Look at it as though it was a photograph and notice how strongly it affects you now. Then just imagine putting it to one side so you can check it again in a moment.

2. Next call to mind four negative experiences with your ex-partner where you felt very definitely upset, or repulsed by them. Perhaps you will think of times when they did something that really offended you or did something that you found hurtful. Make a list of them so you can easily call them to mind.

3. Now run through those four negative memories one at a time in detail as though you were inside each of them re-enacting the moment. See the things you saw, hear the things you heard, and feel completely the negative feelings you felt all over again, like you are actually there.

4. Now spend time going through the memories again and again, one after another, each time making the images a bit bigger, brighter, and more colorful so they are more and more intense. Go through them faster and faster, until the events are overlapping, until there is no break at all between all the worst parts happening over and over again.

5. When you have generated a really strong negative feeling throughout your body, add that picture of yourself when you were in love with your ex alongside all those horrible times and keep running the negative memories.

6. You will feel very different now. Ask yourself how attractive that picture is in this context.

7. When it is no longer attractive, imagine stepping out of all the memories and imagine all the pictures and feelings to do with your ex floating away from you and going off into the past.

Many people only need to do this technique once to feel totally free of their attachments to their old relationship. But if you want to, you can do it carefully and thoroughly again in order to reinforce the effect.

Use the CD Daily

I was once contacted by a lady who had suffered from agoraphobia for many years. She hadn't been out in public on her own since her mid-twenties, and she was living in a violently abusive relationship.

A friend gave her one of my confidence CDs, just like the one you have received with this book. After less than a week, the powerful mind programming techniques had begun to do their work. A few weeks later she flew to Australia on her own. When she returned she had decided to leave her husband and start a new life in another part of the country. She has never looked back. And neither will you . . .

The Confidence Clinic

Frequently Asked Questions

Q. I've set my goals, I've tried the techniques, I've listened to the CD, I'm taking action— and I'm still scared! What am I doing wrong?

Nothing—it sounds like you're doing everything right!

I once saw an interview with Bruce Springsteen where the reporter asked him if he ever got scared before playing concerts in front of huge stadiums, often with more than 50,000 people in the audience.

To my amazement, Springsteen replied, "Never. When I get ready to go on stage, my heart starts pounding, my hands start shaking, my breath goes up into my throat, and I know I am PUMPED and ready to play."

That "pumped and ready to play" feeling (a.k.a. "fear") is the result of the natural release of adrenaline, which occurs any time you step outside of your comfort zone or do something for the very first time. And as long as you're creating confident pictures, talking to yourself in a confident way, and taking daily action even before you're ready, you're doing everything you need to succeed.

Q. How soon can I expect to be more confident?

Do you remember as a child how when you would visit your auntie or granny they would always say, "Ooh, haven't you grown?" Even though you didn't wake up each day feeling taller, inside all sorts of changes were happening.

Because many of the changes you are now making are incremental, your friends, family, and colleagues may become aware of your newly emerging confidence before you do.

Using the techniques in this book and on the CD is a bit different for everyone—some people will see an instant improvement, and others will notice the changes happening a bit more slowly.

Whichever it is with you, keep using the techniques and listening to the CD for at least three weeks. This will not only get you well on the way toward achieving your goals, but may even give you a glimpse beyond what you currently think is possible.

Q. Do I really need to do the 5-Minute Daily Confidence Workout? Can't I just listen to the CD?

How can you live confidently if you begin each day by attacking yourself?

Most people have been practicing beginning each day with a 5-minute daily "feel like crap" workout. They do a quick review of everything that's wrong with their life, then look in the mirror and run themselves down repeatedly. They create a massively negative internal state and associate it with themselves.

The 5-Minute Daily Confidence Workout is there to interrupt the old pattern and begin practicing something new. While listening to the CD on its own will ultimately reprogram your mind, taking the time to reinforce the programming by repeating some of the exercises and doing the daily workout will accelerate the process and help you to feel naturally confident throughout the day.

Q. Actually, my friends say I've become more arrogant since I started reading the book. How do I know if I'm turning into a jerk?

When we change it scares some people, because humans like familiarity. So when we suddenly start standing up for ourselves it seems out of character. Also some people don't want you to become more confident because you become more powerful than they are.

You will know it's working because people will say that you are different. Some will be happy for you and some will feel uncomfortable. The important thing is that in the early stages you are different, although it may take a little while for some of your friends to adjust to the new you.

Also remember, this isn't about "fake it 'til you make it"—it's about changing the pictures and sounds in your head and the way you use your body to become more comfortable in your own skin.

Then, when you've set your BIG goals and begun taking daily action toward achieving them (even before you feel ready), your life will transform.

If your friends are really your friends, they'll still like you as you become more confident, motivated, and successful. And if they start acting jealous, tell them to buy their own copy of this book!

Q. I get so pumped up when I do the techniques, but then I feel all revved up with no place to go. What should I do?

Remember, confidence without action is just a feeling—and action without a clear sense of direction won't necessarily take you where you want to go. If you are feeling like that, it's simply because you haven't created a compelling enough future yet.

Review the sections on setting BIG goals and taking daily action. The goals you set will give you the sense of direction, and the daily action habit will take all those good feelings and put them to work for you.

That way on the days when you can't seem to get the feelings as intense as you're used to, you'll still be carried by the action habit closer and closer to the life of your dreams.

Q. I'm worried that if I start acting more confident than the guys, they won't want to go out with me anymore. Is there a more "female" version of this?

First off, it's not about "acting" confident, it's about practicing the skills of being confident—comfortable and at ease with your body and your life. And in my experience, nothing is more attractive to men OR women than the inner glow that comes from being truly comfortable in your own skin.

Q. I was abused as a child and I still find it difficult to assert myself with certain people. Will these techniques help?

They almost certainly will, but if you are dealing with any sort of past trauma, I highly recommend you begin by seeing a specialist in dealing with it before you begin using the techniques.

In the meantime, as you use the techniques and listen to the CD, it will help you to realize that the past is now over and you can condition yourself to experience more confidence and motivation, regardless of what you may have been through before. Be sure to listen to the CD daily for at least three weeks to reinforce powerful changes in yourself.

Q. It's all right for you—you've got everything you want. I'm sure I'd be confident too if I was famous and successful!

I shared my story in *Change Your Life in Seven Days*, but suffice it to say that I would have loved to have had a book like this when I was growing up. It wasn't until I started learning hypnosis that I began to develop my own confidence, and it wasn't until I'd really developed the habits of confidence, motivation, and action that my life began to change for the better.

If I've achieved anything worthwhile it's been as a result of everything I've shared with you in this book. I still have my challenges and I'm glad because that's how we learn and grow. If I'm lucky I always will—that way I can continue to learn and grow for the rest of my life!

A Final Thought

Years ago, over the course of a week when I was recording my "Stop Smoking" CDs, the sound engineer came up to me during a break looking worried. When I asked him what was wrong, he said he hadn't had a cigarette for several days and he "always smoked."

Was it possible, he asked, that the CD's techniques had affected him, even though he had just been listening casually without intending to change?

There's an old saying that "if you want to learn something, go and teach it." In the course of writing this book, I have noticed my own sense of inner ease and confidence increasing, to the point that my friends have asked me what I'm doing differently. I have also found myself taking action "before I am ready" more often, and the results have been phenomenal.

I wrote this book for you, and I sincerely hope that you find it transforms your life as much as working on it has benefited mine—may your dearest wishes come true!

To your success,
Paul McKenna

Index of Techniques

About the Author

Paul McKenna, PhD, is the best-selling author of *I Can Make You Thin* and *I Can Make You Sleep*. The London *Times* called him "one of the most important modern self-help gurus." Dr. McKenna has helped millions of people lose weight, quit smoking, overcome insomnia, eliminate stress, and increase self-confidence. He has appeared on *The Ellen DeGeneres Show*, *Rachael Ray*, *Good Morning America*, *The Early Show*, *The Dr. Oz Show*, *The Bonnie Hunt Show*, and *Fox and Friends*. His TV shows are regularly watched by hundreds of millions of people in 42 countries around the world. His private clients include rock stars, movie stars, world champion athletes, and royalty. Now he wants to help you!

For more information about Paul McKenna
and his techniques, visit

www.mckenna.com